Real Nurses
Unreal Success

Certified Legal Nurse Consultants^{CM}
Reveal Their Secrets

FIFTH EDITION

Other books and programs by

Vickie L. Milazzo, RN, MSN, JD

CLNC® Certification Program
  (Seminar, Online, DVD and CD)

NACLNC® and Private Apprenticeships
  (Seminar, Online, DVD and CD)

New York Times Bestseller –
Wicked Success Is Inside Every Woman

Core Curriculum for Legal Nurse Consulting®
Textbook, 13th Edition

I Am a Successful CLNC® Success Journal

Create Your Own Magic for CLNC® Success:
  A Unique Book of 91 Devilishly Practical Potions,
  Second Edition

Flash 55 Promotions: 55 FREE Ways to Promote
  Your CLNC® Business, Second Edition

Vickie's *Legal Nurse Consulting* Blog

101 Great Ways to Improve Your Life (coauthor)

Rising to the Top—A Guide to Self-Development
  (coauthored with Jim Rohn and Jack Canfield)

Roadmap to Success (coauthored with Ken Blanchard
and Steven Covey)

Wall Street Journal Bestseller—
Inside Every Woman: Using the 10 Strengths You
  Didn't Know You Had to Get the Career and Life
  You Want Now

UNREAL SUCCESS

REAL NURSES
UNREAL SUCCESS

REAL NURSES

Certified Legal Nurse Consultants[CM]
REVEAL THEIR SECRETS
FIFTH EDITION

Vickie L. Milazzo, RN, MSN, JD, Editor
THE PIONEER OF LEGAL NURSE CONSULTING

> *To the awesome CLNC® consultants whose*
> *dramatic and unique success stories always*
> *inspire me in my vision to revolutionize*
> *nursing careers one RN at a time.*

Real Nurses Unreal Success
Certified Legal Nurse Consultants^{CM}
Reveal Their Secrets
FIFTH EDITION

ISBN-13: 978-1-933216-65-2
ISBN-10: 1-933216-65-4

Editor: Vickie L. Milazzo, RN, MSN, JD

Publisher: Vickie Milazzo Institute, a division of
          Medical-Legal Consulting Institute, Inc.
          5615 Kirby Drive, Suite 425
          Houston, Texas 77005
          713.942.2200
          LegalNurse.com

Formerly titled: *CLNC® Success Stories*

Printed in the United States of America

Printed on acid free paper (∞).

Success Story Contributors

Becky Mungai, RN, BA, CLNC, *Florida,* 27

Lisa Panish, RN, MSN, ARNP-BC, CLNC, *Florida,* 188

Melanie V. Paquette, RN, BSN, CLNC, *Texas,* 222

Leana Peterson-Leaf, RN, CLNC, *Illinois,* 123

Susan Porter, RNC, BS, CLNC, *South Carolina,* 237

Carol Riley, RN, MHA, CNAA, HFA, CLNC, *Indiana,* 78

Barbara Rose, RN, CLNC, *Texas,* 138

Tanya Sanderson, RN, BSN, RCIS, CLNC, *Tennessee,* 100

Heidi Santiago, RN, CLNC, *New York,* 61

Arlene Santiago-Tribbett, RN, BSN, CLNC, *New Jersey,* 57

Judia Sarich, RN, BSN, CLNC, *Texas,* 217

Suzi Sharp, RN, BSN, CLNC, *Washington,* 231

Jeannie Shoeman, RN, BS, CLNC, *Iowa,* 200

Kathy Silay, RN, CLNC, *Illinois,* 37

Jan M. Skadberg, RN, BSPA, CLNC, *West Virginia,* 213

Guyolyn Smith-Ousterhout, RNC, CPUR, CLNC, *Mississippi,* 150

Carmen Stine, RN, BSN, CCM, CLP, CLNC, *Delaware,* 22

Fredda Thomson, RN, CLNC, *South Carolina,* 204

Kathy Thompson, RN, CLNC, *Ohio,* 162

Michelle Tucker, RN, MSN, CLNC, *Florida,* 136

Teresa C. Vitale, RN, CCM, CLNC, *California,* 59

Ann Wiseman, RN, CLNC, *Maryland,* 191

Contents

2 Take the Fast Track to Financial Freedom

3 Use Vickie's Proven Strategies for Your Own CLNC® Success

Triumph Over Any Personal Challenge

5 Make More Than a Living, Make a *Difference*

You're Ready for CLNC® *Success!*

12 Things Nursing Taught You About Owning a Business

by Vickie L. Milazzo, RN, MSN, JD

When I started out as an RN, I had no idea I was really preparing myself to become an entrepreneur.

Have you ever wondered whether you're cut out to be an entrepreneur? Many of the Certified Legal Nurse Consultants^{CM} featured in this book wondered if their nursing careers had prepared them to start and succeed in their own CLNC® practice. Yet each and every one of them has succeeded, often beyond their wildest dreams. They all learned that even the most routine nursing job is full of life lessons that apply to the business world. They took those lessons—along with all they learned from my trademark CLNC® Certification Program—and transformed their nursing careers. And you can do the same thing!

1

When I started out as an RN, I had no idea I was really preparing myself to become an entrepreneur. Yet my first job as an intensive care nurse in a major medical center started the process of preparing me for business success. Subsequent jobs reinforced those early messages. I invite you to look closely at your own nursing career and discover the lessons that will help you succeed as a CLNC® consultant.

Success Lesson 1
Find Your Passion and Turn It into a Business

"Choose a job you love and you will never have to work a day in your life." —Confucius

As much as I loved my work with critically ill patients and their families, my inner voice told me I wouldn't be working in a hospital forever. As a young RN, the vision of myself working in the ICU at age 40, 50 or 60 just wouldn't come into focus.

With only six years of nursing experience, I left the hospital and started my legal nurse consulting business. From there, I listened to my inner voice and reconnected with my first passion—teaching. At age 8, I spent hours every day teaching an imaginary class. Today I am privileged to teach, coach and mentor RNs to live their career dreams as CLNC® consultants. I turned my passion into a business, and since then I haven't worked a single day.

Listen to your inner voice, and you will find your passion. Many RNs have reconnected to their passion through legal nurse consulting, a choice unknown to them before they took the CLNC® Certification Program.

Success Lesson 2
You Have the Power to Take Control of Your Career Destiny

P atients heal faster when they take control of their health and practice healthy habits. Even the smallest positive action can give a patient a sense of control and empower the healing process.

I learned this lesson time and again as I struggled to gain control of my own nursing career. Each time I refused to give in to the frustrations of working within the healthcare system and took a positive step on my own, I felt better. With every step I grew, I thrived and I came up with new ideas to further my sense of control and satisfaction.

The same is true about your career. You have the power to practice the healthy habits essential to take control of your career destiny. Educate yourself about the steps to achieving career health, including new career options like becoming a Certified Legal Nurse Consultant^CM. Then take action on those steps. You really can take control of your career destiny.

> *You have the power to practice the healthy habits essential to take control of your career destiny.*

Success Lesson 3
Don't Give In to Fear

"Fear is the mind-killer." —Frank Herbert, *Dune*

As a nurse, I frequently treated patients who had the same progressive disease, yet experienced dramatically different outcomes. We all have known patients who lived years after their predicted demise and other patients who should have lived but didn't because they gave up or didn't want to live. The fact that so many elderly patients die within months of losing a spouse is a solid example of the mind-body connection. In almost every case, the patients who died too soon had given in to fear.

There's also a mind-success connection that will influence the health of your career. When I give in to fear, I become the biggest obstacle to my success. That was true when I started my business in 1982 and it's true today.

Fear will paralyze you instantly. Practice mind control and exercise your mind daily for positive thinking. Shake off your negative thinking and lack of confidence.

Don't wait for an MI to stop inhaling the toxic smoke of fear. Don't let fear be the reason you don't live your career dreams. Always remember the mind-set of the patients who live and the patients who die.

Success Lesson 4
Nurses Can Do Anything

As nurses most of us have brought patients back to life. We all can recall at least one miracle story—a case where, with our help, a patient survived against all odds.

Whenever I face a business crisis, I remind myself, "I'm a nurse and nurses can do anything." I've repeated this same message since 1982, and it has helped me overcome every obstacle.

If you can heal sick patients and handle life-threatening emergencies as easily as you make your bed in the morning, you really can do anything—especially something as straightforward as starting a CLNC® business.

Success Lesson 5
What's Hard Today
Will Be Easy Tomorrow

I needed extensive education and training just to qualify for my first nursing job. All the lessons from that job helped prepare me for the next. Each successive nursing position required new and different skills necessitating more training and education.

The same applies to owning a business. Today I easily and successfully handle things that seemed impossible when I started out. But that's because

'I'm a nurse and nurses can do anything.' I've repeated this same message since 1982, and it has helped me overcome every obstacle.

I've been in training for what I do now ever since I became a nurse.

If you're frustrated with your nursing career, don't feel like you've thrown your life away. No experience or job is a waste. Everything you have done has trained you to pursue your dream of becoming an independent CLNC® consultant. Your nursing training and experience were the first step. Start the next step of your training today, and you will be writing your CLNC® success story before you know it.

Nursing has prepared you well. The nursing process doesn't just apply to patients. It applies to any business situation.

Success Lesson 6
The Nursing Process Is Your Friend

When I left clinical nursing, I thought I could set aside the nursing process forever. I couldn't have been more wrong. Business requires that same process—assessment, diagnosis, planning, implementation and evaluation. Every project I take on requires me to assess the possibilities and needs, diagnose the problems, plan how to achieve my goals, implement the plan and evaluate my results.

Nursing has prepared you well. The nursing process doesn't just apply to patients. It applies to any business situation. You will thank your nursing instructors for this one. Every time you review a medical-related case, interview with an attorney or face a challenge in running your business, you will rely on the nursing process they taught you.

Success Lesson 7
Act Quickly and Decisively

As a nurse, I learned that seconds made a difference in patient outcome. That's true for nurses in any specialty. I rarely had lots of time to ponder or brood over a clinical decision.

I have applied the same principle of acting quickly and decisively in business, too. Am I always correct? No. Do I make mistakes? Yes. Yet because of my nursing experience, I'm never paralyzed into inaction and I've been able to make the most of numerous opportunities I would have missed without acting quickly.

Don't miss your chance to succeed. Learn to act quickly and decisively, and you will create your amazing future as a CLNC® consultant.

Success Lesson 8
What You Focus on Is Where You Will Yield Results

In nursing I was often overwhelmed by short staffing, heavy caseloads and lack of support from hospital administration. I soon learned to triage and focus on what I needed to do to heal patients in this less-than-ideal environment. Nursing taught me that where I focus my time is where I yield results.

That skill comes in handy in business. It's as important to triage and prioritize your actions in

Because of my nursing experience, I'm never paralyzed into inaction.

Nursing taught me that where I focus my time is where I yield results.

business as it is when working with patients. Every day I'm confronted with dozens of challenges, five things that must be done at once and 20 new creative ideas for my business, but I rarely panic. The organizational and multitasking skills I learned as a nurse have served me well.

When you start your CLNC® business, you will not receive any extra hours in the day. In fact, the days will feel shorter. Even the general public knows that working conditions for RNs are worse than ever. Your ability to focus on what's really important under these conditions is the perfect preparation for your successful CLNC® business.

> *The organizational and multitasking skills I learned as a nurse have served me well.*

> *Your ability to focus on what's really important... is the perfect preparation for your successful CLNC® business.*

Success Lesson 9
This Is Just Business, It's Not Breast Cancer

Ministering to patients and family members helped me put life, with all its problems and challenges, into perspective. Today when I overreact to a problem or feel I'm in crisis, I think of sick and dying patients and remind myself, "Now fighting for your life is a *real* problem."

In business I've had lots of ups and downs. When the down moments come, I remind myself, "This is business—not breast cancer." This helps me focus positively on solving the problem rather than embarking on a pity party. I've thrown plenty of those "parties," and they never solved a single business problem.

As you grow your CLNC® business, it helps to ask, "So what if this month is not as successful as I planned?" or "So what if my best attorney-client retires?" and to remember it's just business, not breast cancer.

Success Lesson 10
Illness Can Wake You Up

A s a nurse I treated many patients who only began to live after they almost died. We've all had patients who said they're glad they got sick, because while they were well, they weren't living the life they wanted. The health crisis forced them to wake up, reassess their lives, decide what was truly important to them and go for it.

Not every day is a healthy business day. Some days I wake up to a "disease" challenge in my business. Surprisingly, it's the business ills and mistakes that often awaken me to creative ways of injecting my business with new life.

If your career is facing a health crisis, this is your opportunity to wake up and change things for the better. Legal nurse consulting is one way to restore the health of your career.

Success Lesson 11
Business Is Personal

E ven though technical skills are vital for an RN, the relationships with patients and their families were what mattered most to me. Those relationships paid off one day when

Surprisingly, it's the business ills and mistakes that often awaken me to creative ways of injecting my business with new life.

I made a mistake. Because of our relationship, the patient requested that I continue being his nurse despite my error.

Just like nursing, business is personal. I have all the technical skills to lead my seminars and run my business. In fact, at this stage I could hand off some of those responsibilities to others. But I still teach every CLNC® 6-Day Certification Seminar we offer and coach students daily because those relationships are what I thrive on. No one else could replicate my relationship with each and every nurse whose life I touch. As a result, most of our business comes from referrals by practicing CLNC® consultants who graduated from our educational programs.

Legal nurse consulting is a service business where you will apply the same relationship principles you learned in nursing to your attorney-clients and prospects. Provide quality service and excellent work product that no other legal nurse consultant can replicate, and soon you'll feel like you're in a short-staffing situation all over again.

Success Lesson 12
Healthy Patients Take Care of Themselves

We've all worked with healthy and unhealthy patients, and we've seen the effects of poor health habits on the human body. The health of a pregnant woman

> *I still teach every CLNC® 6-Day Certification Seminar we offer and coach students daily because those relationships are what I thrive on.*

is often dramatically reflected in the health of her offspring.

To run a successful company you must enjoy an optimal state of health. Give yourself permission to take care of yourself. I love my business, but I love myself more. After all, without a healthy me, I couldn't muster the energy to give 110% to my clients and employees every day.

My Personal Prescription for Optimal Health

▸ **Exercise**—My goal is to exercise at least five days a week. I love hiking, hot yoga and working with weights.

▸ **Massage**—A once-a-week massage renews my energy.

▸ **Vacation**—I schedule 12 weeks of vacation for myself every year.

▸ **Time with spouse and family**—Time for love. In a herd of elephants when one falls, the others pick him up. I love being surrounded by my own family of elephants.

▸ **Daily prayer and meditation**—I'm most creative in the silence.

▸ **Weight control**—I eat pure, unprocessed foods with occasional treats like popcorn at the movies.

▸ **Supplements**—Flaxseed, green tea, vitamins and antioxidants are part of my daily regimen.

To run a successful company you must enjoy an optimal state of health. Give yourself permission to take care of yourself.

> ▸ **Fun**—I schedule something fun at least twice a week, including time for things I love—reading, walks with my husband, our whirlpool, theater and musicals.

> ▸ **Sleep**—I get 7-8 hours of sleep per night, not per week.

> ▸ **Taking Sunday off**—I don't even make my bed.

> ▸ **Working my passion**—I revolutionize nursing careers—one RN at a time.

Write a prescription for your own optimal health physically, spiritually and emotionally—and follow it. Then you'll have the energy and vitality to enjoy your career as a Certified Legal Nurse Consultant℠.

Every lesson I learned from nursing, I apply to my business today. You've already learned similar lessons yourself. You don't need another hospital job to help you succeed in business. Take a moment to revel in all nursing has taught you. Then read the CLNC® success stories we've compiled in this book.

Like me, the nurses who wrote these true stories recognized what nursing had taught them and applied those lessons to building their dream careers. Follow their example—take all you've learned as a nurse and all you will learn from my proven CLNC® Certification Program, and apply it diligently to your legal nurse consulting practice. I promise you, your success will multiply.

Write a prescription for your own optimal health physically, spiritually and emotionally —and follow it.

Imagine, Believe, Achieve Your New *Life* as a CLNC® Consultant

A $1,000,000 CLNC® Business Is Attainable. Go for It–I Did

by Suzanne E. Arragg, RN, BSN, CDONA/LTC, CLNC, California

> *This was the most rewarding experience of my whole nursing career.*

I have been a registered nurse since 1985, but seven years ago my path began a slow and steady 180-degree turn. I'd been the director of nursing services in a skilled nursing facility (SNF) for just under a year, when my dad spotted a classified ad in our local newspaper. A defense law firm was seeking a legal nurse consultant. I learned that this firm was legal counsel for three of the top five long term care corporations in the country. My initial response was, "I don't have that kind of training."

My director position included being on call 24 hours per day, 7 days a week. Besides this grueling job, I was going through a nasty divorce and had primary custody of my three children, ages 4, 6 and 8, with no child support. To top it off, I found out I needed a hysterectomy for a pre-cancerous condition. I was depressed, sleep-deprived, stressed, short-tempered, financially upside-down and in debt. A financial advisor told me there was no way I could retire, even with Social Security. I felt like I was on a sinking ship.

Three weeks after my dad showed me the ad, I submitted my resume. I figured I had nothing to lose, and it's always good to keep my interviewing skills fresh. My SNF colleagues saw the same ad and submitted their resumes, too.

My Persistence Landed Me My First Assignment

I knew consistent follow-up was a must, once you have submitted a resume. Over the next five weeks, I had many pleasant conversations with the chief partner's legal secretary. I got to know her on a first-name basis, and she told me he was in trial and to keep calling. I also left voice mail messages for the attorney. Finally, he called me.

Obviously, he knew I was persistent, and at the first interview he could tell I presented well and I had the knowledge he needed to litigate his cases.

Within a half-hour, we agreed on my hourly rate, which was more than I was then making, and I left with my first long term care case. Needless to say, my colleagues never got a call and were shocked at my success, especially since they had 15 years' experience on me.

This first case was voluminous—more than 30,000 pages of medical records spanning 20 years. I worked with the chief partner and one of his associates through the entire legal process. My tasks included organizing, reconstructing and analyzing the medical records, defining standards of nursing care, identifying state and federal regulatory deficiencies, identifying appropriate testifying experts, educating the attorney, assisting with trial preparation, and developing and designing demonstrative evidence used in the trial, just to name a few.

This was the most rewarding experience of my whole nursing career. I was intellectually challenged, and there was nothing mundane about the medical-legal process. I was so impacted by this experience I was convinced this was my future and a way to earn enough income to get out of debt. With my parents' support, I attended Vickie's CLNC® 6-Day Certification Seminar and became a Certified Legal Nurse Consultant℠.

The day I got home from the seminar, I called my attorney-client, who had just received the jury verdict: We had won this landmark case. I was ecstatic and he was absolutely thrilled. He couldn't thank me enough for educating and assisting him with my nursing expertise. He said he would refer all his

We had won this landmark case. I was ecstatic and the attorney was absolutely thrilled. He couldn't thank me enough.

Vickie is incredibly motivating. She knows how to speak to a nurse's heart.

cases to me. I thanked him profusely and informed him of my new CLNC® status. He became a very high-volume client for me.

My CLNC® Certification Made All the Difference in My Full-Time Success

Vickie's CLNC® Certification Program and *Core Curriculum for Legal Nurse Consulting*® textbook expanded my limited understanding of the legal nurse consultant's role. They helped me improve my reports and presentation style, and provided me with the business strategies needed to become an independent business owner.

Vickie is incredibly motivating. She knows how to speak to a nurse's heart. Her endless energy emanates through her words. Throughout the CLNC® 6-Day Certification Seminar, I could see she was totally engrossed in what she was teaching. I identified with her passion, but I also realized I didn't exhibit passion like she did. I made a commitment to express my passion as Vickie does and to maintain an upbeat and positive attitude in my life and in my business. This attitude encourages my attorney-clients as well. You make a better overall impression by always appearing confident, cheerful and optimistic. This helps keep your clients happy and willing to promote your CLNC® services. That's another thing I learned from Vickie.

My number one rule for securing repeat business is being open to and listening for the attorney's needs in each case I accept. Attorney-specific, case-specific is my motto!

Last year my firm exceeded $1 million in revenue.

I've found my passion, I'm actually fulfilling it and it's providing me with a stimulating and rewarding lifestyle.

For the next three years, I continued to work as a director of nursing services in another skilled nursing facility and ran my part-time CLNC® business from home. Sometimes it was a family affair, with my children working for me. All three of them have filed and scanned medical records. I tried to instill the entrepreneurial spirit and some business savvy as well. During this time, in addition to performing the same services I started with, I added attending mediation conferences, assisting the attorney in preparing MD and nurse testifying experts, and participating in risk management seminars for long term care corporations.

Meeting the Challenges of Growth Brought Me Even Greater Successes

While still a part-time CLNC® consultant, I was able to buy a home, eliminate financial dependence on my parents and provide for my three children, including enabling them to participate in sports and many other extracurricular activities they couldn't enjoy previously. During my transition from part time to full time four years ago, my legal nurse consulting revenues were $85,000.

When I reached my goal of quitting the SNF and becoming a full-time Certified Legal Nurse Consultant^{CM}, I held a wine-and-cheese open house to celebrate the opening of my new office and to share my success with friends and family, and current and potential attorney-clients. About six months after I went full time, I took Vickie's advice and added my first employee, who's still with me. I also subcon-

> *Today I can do the things I only dreamed of doing when I retire.*

> *Vickie Milazzo Institute provides all the tools you need to get started. Vickie shows you how to make your CLNC® business fun and rewarding.*

tracted with four CLNC® consultants. That year I massively exceeded my goal of grossing $200,000.

Two short years later, my business had expanded by adding more office space, two employees and another CLNC® subcontractor. As a result, my firm doubled its revenues.

As the business continued to grow, I refined our services and added more qualified, high-caliber individuals. I now have a 3,200-square-foot office and a total of ten employees—four nurses plus support and administrative staff. Having the in-house expertise of Certified Legal Nurse Consultants℠ who share my vision is truly exciting.

Business keeps rolling in because we deliver a superior work product to our clients. This generates a prompt response from the attorney: "Suzanne, this is awesome. We can do big things with this." Last year my firm exceeded $1 million in revenue.

Today I Can *Do* Things I Only Dreamed of Doing When I Retire

While this kind of financial success is not necessarily the primary goal, it's exciting that I've found my passion, I'm actually fulfilling it and it's providing me with a stimulating and rewarding lifestyle. My eldest is going to college next year. I'm prepared for that expensive college tuition and I never thought I would be.

Balancing the business and my family is still a challenge. At least financially I have the freedom to spend more time with them, knowing and feeling comfortable that someone's still running the office, especially if want to take off in the middle of the week. Today I can *do* the things I only dreamed of doing when I retire.

I have always had a deep faith in God and commitment to prayer. The Lord has blessed me with the ability to discern what is important in my life and has given me the strength to work hard and learn all I can.

Professionally, I wouldn't be where I am today without becoming a Certified Legal Nurse Consultant^{CM}. There's no other program out there like Vickie's. There is simply no competition. She and Vickie Milazzo Institute provide all the tools you need to get started. She shows you how to make your CLNC® business fun and rewarding, not only financially but in other ways. Being a CLNC® consultant represents a high level of professionalism. The *National Alliance of Certified Legal Nurse Consultants* embraces networking instead of competition between nurses. I've seen this industry grow and I think it will continue to grow. It's up to CLNC® business owners to uplift the nursing profession and maintain that positive attitude, knowing that there's enough work out there for all of us.

I come to the *NACLNC®* Conferences for my annual boost. It's my yearly reminder of the power of nurses and the power of nursing in the community. I also get to see Vickie, take part in some fascinating sessions and network with more than 1,200 nurses.

If I could say one thing to my RN peers, I'd advise them to take their fear and do something

Vickie walks the walk. She's an inspiration, not only as a nurse who pioneered a new industry but also as a keen-minded, successful business-woman who openly shares her secrets.

with it. Evaluate what you want for your life, embrace the fear and then go for it. The next step is following a marketing plan to make sure the business is growing, new cases are coming in and new prospects are hearing about you. You can never take your current clients for granted. Customer service has to be number one. Every single member of my team knows the importance of that. We're human; we make little mistakes. But if you're always there for your attorney-clients, always answering questions, meeting deadlines and following up, those minor human errors will be no biggie.

The CLNC® Mentoring Program is absolutely crucial to your growth into a mature CLNC® consultant. Vickie and her staff are always there for you. No other program is actually there to lift you up when you're down, to provide the support that is so necessary to becoming successful.

Vickie Is My Inspiration as a Successful, Savvy Entrepreneur

Vickie walks the walk. She's an inspiration, not only as a nurse who pioneered a new industry but also as a keen-minded, successful businesswoman who openly shares her secrets. Vickie's wisdom and her generosity with that wisdom have made me stronger, more passionate and driven to succeed for my family and for my personal growth.

Vickie lives her motto, "Revolutionizing Nursing Careers One RN at a Time." I'm a categorical example of one of those careers she revolutionized.

What stuck with me the most was her statement that you are a nurse and you can do anything. I truly took that motto to heart.

I always remember where I came from and that I started my CLNC® business from my bedroom. Rebounding from divorce, depression and financial inadequacy was tough, but I have grown tremendously as a person. Today I'm very appreciative that I don't have to work in my bedroom anymore. I love my life. I love my career. I spend time with my children. I consistently bring in a comfortable six-figure income and it just keeps getting better.

Thank you, Vickie, for giving me the motivation and education to become a CLNC® success.

> *I love my career. I spend time with my children. I consistently bring in a comfortable six-figure income—and it just keeps getting better.*

I Created a Potential Half-Million-Dollar-a-Year CLNC® Business Through My Belief and Vickie's Preparation

by Carmen Stine, RN, BSN, CCM, CLP, CLNC, Delaware

I have been an RN for well over 35 years and became a Certified Legal Nurse Consultant last year. I now have my own very successful CLNC® business.

I learned about legal nurse consulting by seeing Vickie Milazzo Institute ads for 15 years. During that time, I thought of becoming a Certified Legal Nurse Consultant but the timing was never right for one reason or another. Early in my career I felt I wasn't experienced enough and midway through my career, life was happening with family and financial responsibilities. Last year, I saw the ad with Vickie's photo once again and something just clicked inside me. Instinctively, I knew this was my next career move. Having worked in the home healthcare field for seven years, I loved the autonomy, the field work and the attachment to my patients and their families. However, I was getting quite tired of the constant bureaucratic demands. I was at the brink of burnout so the timing for me to pursue a career change was right. I quickly enrolled in the VIP CLNC® Business System with financing.

I watched the CLNC® Certification Home-Study Program DVDs for a total of 65 hours and soon scheduled my CLNC® Certification Exam. Throughout the process of my newfound education, I was excited at the prospect of using my extensive nursing knowledge and experience, creating a business of my own, educating attorneys and others on medical issues (I love to teach) and continuing to help people.

I took the CLNC® Certification Exam at a Prometric Testing Center, and I was so happy when the screen on the computer displayed my passing score that I cried for about 10 minutes. I was now a Certified Legal Nurse Consultant℠. I went home, immediately put all my marketing materials together and mailed out 25 packets. Within three days, an attorney at the biggest law firm in my county called me to meet with him and his paralegal. He was very excited that I was so close. This firm does only personal injury and medical-malpractice cases. A few days later, I went to my first attorney meeting to sell my CLNC® services. Unbeknownst to me, there were nine attorneys, three paralegals and three executive assistants waiting for me at this meeting. If this was a test for how I would do under pressure, I am proud to say I passed with flying colors.

During my interview, I focused on them and how I could help solve their problems (just like Vickie teaches). I asked several questions about what their biggest challenges were and how they were currently dealing with those challenges. I then explained how my CLNC® services would enhance

> *I addressed each of their challenges with confirmation that 'this is why you need me'. I walked out of the office with nine cases to review.*

what they were already doing because I had the benefit of knowing the ins and outs of the hospital structure, workflows, hierarchy, etc. I emphasized that I have always analyzed, assessed, evaluated and made critical decisions about nursing and medical care. I addressed each of their challenges with confirmation that "this is why you need me" (sound familiar?). I emphasized the unique involvement of the paralegals and executive assistants and shared how I could help free them to focus on their respective duties. After 45 minutes, I walked out of the office with nine cases to review. I worked on the three most urgent cases first and returned them within five days. My attorney-clients were very impressed at my timeliness, professionalism, ability to work with their staff and the quality of the reports I provided. I completed the other six reviews within seven business days and again they were very impressed. After the initial reviews, I helped prepare those nine cases for litigation and acquired new cases as well.

Incredibly in the first two cases, I discovered tampering of the medical records. The two attorneys working these cases were awed at my discovery. Both cases settled for significantly more than was previously anticipated. The ability to detect medical tampering has catapulted me to success with this law firm.

I was not at all afraid to put myself out there because I felt so confident with my clinical background, my experience and the education I received from Vickie in the CLNC® Certification Program.

Having prepared myself to market also helped me feel confident. I think preparation is key to anyone's success. I know in my soul that I have a lot to offer any attorney who is willing to work with me, and with that mindset, I can't fail. My standard of excellence gives me great confidence as well. You have to believe in yourself and what you are offering in order for others to believe in you too. Being focused, self-directed and clear in what you want to accomplish is absolutely crucial for success.

Transitioning from my full-time home healthcare job, where I was earning $120,000/yr to full-time CLNC® consultant at $225/hr took me exactly four weeks. I consult with 12 attorneys in this firm, billing $8,000-10,000 a week on average. I have built a potential $500,000-600,000 a year business in the last six months. My goal is to create a $1 million business within the next two years.

My life has changed forever, in more ways than I can include here. These are just some of the highlights:

- ▸ I work from home: no commute, no traffic, no weather issues, no burnout!
- ▸ I built a brand-new 10,000 sq. ft. home.
- ▸ I created my own financial freedom.
- ▸ I built a successful CLNC® business with a high profile in the legal community.
- ▸ I gained an abundance of new friends and business associates.

Of course, no success is possible without a support system. First and foremost, I thank God every day for my blessings. Many thanks to my husband

I consult with 12 attorneys billing $8,000-10,000 a week.

I have built a potential $500,000-600,000 a year business.

and my mother for their endless support. Equal appreciation to Vickie for the amazing preparation I have been so privileged to obtain. As Vickie says: "We are nurses and we can do anything!®"

"My life has changed forever. I built a brand-new 10,000 sq. ft. home."

In My 4th Month I Billed $16,000 and Became a Full-Time CLNC® Consultant

by Becky Mungai, RN, BA, CLNC

I am thrilled to have the opportunity to share the success of my CLNC® career. I could tell my story a million times because it's so exciting to have finally achieved all of my professional goals.

I grew up with the aspiration of becoming an obstetrician. I entered college as a pre-med student and it wasn't long before I realized how challenging being a doctor and a hands-on parent would be. I wanted to be a mom more than anything. I decided to change direction towards my other interests, teaching and psychology. I got a B.A. in psychology, a minor in coaching and completed all my teaching courses but quit during student teaching. I didn't love it. I couldn't deny that I loved medicine, so I became a nurse.

I'm 47 now, and I've felt like I shortchanged myself my entire life and hadn't reached my full potential. I wanted to achieve a certain status and financial level, and I never got that from nursing. As an ER nurse, I had a tremendous amount of responsibility and yet I was treated as insignificant compared to the physicians. I graduated at the top of my high school class and received a full college scholarship with early entrance and honors on

And if I was going to invest in myself, I was going all the way. I ordered the VIP CLNC® Business System.

Every day is spent doing exactly what I want to be doing. I finally feel like I'm getting the professional respect I've sought my entire life.

admission. I graduated summa cum laude with two degrees and my teaching coursework completed. It was always frustrating to have so much education, so little respect and such minimal compensation. I was sick of it.

Vickie's Big Smile Beckoned Me to Escape a "Toxic" ER Environment

I decided to make a change. In Oregon, I had an awesome job working dayshift and basically running my own cosmetic laser business with a talented and well-respected plastic surgeon who compensated me well, gave me autonomy and respected my intellect. And while I appreciated this opportunity, it still didn't meet my list of criteria for success. I soon grew bored and the sunshine and water were calling me, so we put two kids in college, took our little one and moved to Florida. We bought a big, beautiful house on the water with a huge mortgage (actually a moderate mortgage but adding hurricane insurance made it huge). My husband, following his heart and desire to find his passion, left a successful corporate-America career and started a video production company.

I expected my nursing salary in Florida to be about the same as Oregon, but it was only half as much. The panhandle of Florida offered sunshine and white sand beaches but the unique situation I had in Oregon was not available. I went back to the Peds ED. I love kids and emergency care but in addition to the low pay, I was dismayed by the sketchy quality of medical care. I was not proud to

I'm not only being treated like an equal, I'm being treated as a tremendous asset.

be part of that ED. The other nurses felt the same way and their response was to constantly complain and create a "toxic" environment. It was sucking the life out of me.

I needed to get out of that situation, and I felt like this was my last chance to make a change. I had always been interested in law and started searching for a law program. But I had a ten-year old, and if I went to law school, I'd still have to work full-time and I'd shortchange him. I just wasn't willing to make that sacrifice. My list of criteria became: to be appropriately compensated for my knowledge and work ethic; to work from home (my office looks out onto the bay with dolphins swimming by); to never work another holiday or weekend; to have the freedom to care for my child when he is sick; to go on field trips; to volunteer in the classroom; and to be respected and commended for my expertise.

For years I'd seen Vickie's smiling picture in the ads for her CLNC® Certification Program. I saw her program as the perfect combination of my two interests; law and medicine. When I realized how comprehensive her training was, I ordered everything she offered. It was my belief that if one nurse could do this, I could! And if I was going to invest in myself, I was going all the way. I was setting myself up for success. I ordered the VIP CLNC® Business System.

Before I went to the CLNC® 6-Day Certification Seminar, I studied the CLNC® Certification Program on DVDs and the *Core Curriculum for Legal Nurse Consulting®* textbook. I did this for two rea-

> *Between the attorneys and Vickie Milazzo Institute, I am ecstatic!*

sons: to decrease my test-taking anxiety and to get the most out of the week-long seminar. I know that anxiety makes it difficult to absorb information and like I said, I was setting myself up for success. I had all the information from the DVDs–now I wanted to solidify it and grab all the nuances that would be offered at Vickie's seminar.

By the time I walked into the CLNC® 6-Day Certification Seminar, I was already prepared to take the CLNC® Certification Exam. I used those six days–plus the *NACLNC®* Apprenticeship–to fine tune.

As a side benefit I even lost 25 pounds when I started my CLNC® business. It was effortless and I think it was because I'm so happy. Every day is spent doing exactly what I want to be doing. I finally feel like I'm getting the professional respect I've sought my entire life. I'm not only being treated like an equal, I'm being treated as a tremendous asset. The attorneys need me and they respect my intelligence. They pump me up constantly. Gone are the days of the "toxic" hospital environment.

Between the attorneys and Vickie Milazzo Institute, I am ecstatic! Vickie gives you all the tools you need, and the Institute holds your hand every step of the way. When something great happens, they're there to cheer you on, as if they are family. That's unheard of, especially in nursing. As a Certified Legal Nurse Consultant℠, I finally feel like I've arrived.

I Branded My CLNC® Business Like Vickie Taught and Networked My Way to Success

The first thing I did was put together a promotional packet with the brochure from the CLNC® Marketing LaunchBox, along with my resume and a list of my CLNC® services.

For 23 years I had worked in pediatric emergency and attended over 2,000 deliveries as the primary neonatal nurse. I'm confident of my knowledge in these areas. In addition, I found that my specialties, birth trauma and pediatric emergency trauma, are highly litigious. So I did an Internet search on birth trauma attorneys. I'd read an attorney's bio and if I had something in common with him, I'd call. If an attorney played college basketball, went to Phillips Academy, was a Theta or went to Whitman College, I'd call them. I used that connection to get past the gatekeeper.

The first time I tried this I called the attorney's office and said, "Hi, this is Becky Mungai. Is Kirby in? We went to Whitman College together." The secretary didn't ask any questions. She just put me through. That attorney's partner became my first case. While Christmas shopping I got a call from an attorney who said, "Kirby gave me your number. I need you and another L&D nurse to look at a case and give me a verbal opinion." All it took was that one attorney's call to fuel my energy for my CLNC® business. I had my first case and my first subcontracting opportunity.

I recently returned from a legal conference in Nevada. I came home with seven new attorney-clients and 11 cases.

I currently work with attorneys in 19 states. I'm on track to achieve six figures!

I Billed $16,000 in My Fourth Month

The day I came back from the CLNC® 6-Day Certification Seminar, I went half time at the hospital. I was determined to invest time in my CLNC® business. I couldn't work full time and start my business or someone would be shortchanged, and it wasn't going to be my child.

Soon I was billing so many hours as a CLNC® consultant–$16,000 in my fourth month alone!– that I could no longer work at the hospital.

I recently returned from a legal conference in Nevada. It was my sixth conference this year. I came home with seven new attorney-clients and 11 cases. In addition, I currently have several cases in progress and work with attorneys in 19 states. I'm scheduled for three more conferences in the next few months and have been asked to present at a legal seminar. I'm on track to achieve six figures!

With each new case, I learn more about managing a successful CLNC® practice. In one early case, I was talking to the attorney and he mentioned that he already had his team in place and didn't need anyone else. Nevertheless, the attorney went on to describe a case over the phone. I gave him some questions to ask his expert and the defendant. When I followed up to see how it went he said he had forgotten to ask some of the questions. He responded with, "Why don't I send you some of the records to see what you think. Just put me on the clock." What he sent was 18 pages. For a couple of weeks, I couldn't think of a single thing

I hadn't already told him. But he'd said to put him on the clock, and I was determined to find something! Finally, I decided to put what I had already told him in chronology format to see if anything else popped out at me. Sure enough, I discovered a tampering issue. The attorney was so busy, he didn't comment–but more than a month later he called and said, "That tampering issue you found blew this case wide open. All of a sudden we have additional discovery. Thank you so much!"

I Love Making Connections and They Always Pay Off

I love connecting with new attorneys. It's my favorite part of this business. I met with one attorney who's very well respected in town. She has her own nurse consultant working in-house, but she agreed to meet with me anyway. I asked her why, and she said, "I just like how you sound on the phone." As a result of meeting her, she has referred two attorneys to me and I've done a lot of work with one of them. She had a tough case several months ago and emailed me for emotional support. Our relationship continues to grow.

I was recently requested to fly to Houston to teach an attorney about newborn resuscitation for one of her cases. She was flying in from the West Coast. We met with another attorney I do cases for and her partner who is an anesthesiologist. We spent a couple days teaching, working up the case and brainstorming some of my other cases. She is one of my favorite attorney-clients.

The unlimited mentoring with the CLNC® Mentors is phenomenal.

The VIP CLNC® Business System Is the Nordstrom of Legal Nurse Consulting

The CLNC® Mentors give great advice and always lead me in the right direction. It's the support network I had been looking for in nursing and had yet to find.

The first thing I received from the Institute was the free Success DVD and the CLNC® Success Stories book. I watched the Success DVD and read the Success Stories book. Then when I'd go for a walk, I'd create my CLNC® Success Story in my head. I believe that if you think you'll be successful, you will. Vickie teaches the same thing. When she says, "We are successful CLNC® consultants," she's putting that in our heads–dress for success, act successful and you'll be successful. It'll all happen–and it did.

If you have a choice of going to the best four-year college to prepare for your career, would you take a correspondence course instead? No, you'd choose the best, and that's what Vickie provides. I absolutely recommend the VIP CLNC® Business System. The added cost of the VIP CLNC® Business System, when you divide it out over five years, comes down to pennies basically, but you're investing in yourself by getting it all. As a VIP you also feel more successful while you're in the program.

The unlimited mentoring with the CLNC® Mentors is phenomenal. I tend to hold onto a problem too long–I want to solve it myself and then I panic because I need the answer right this second. The CLNC® Mentors get right back to me. They support me all the way. They never act like I'm taking up their time. They want to know, "Have I answered all your questions? Do you need anything else?"

I feel like they "have my back." They want me to succeed. There is no competition. It's all about complementing my efforts and pumping me up. The CLNC® Mentors give great advice and always lead me in the right direction. It's the support network I had been looking for in nursing and had yet to find.

Vickie gives you all the tools. She's dotted every "i" and crossed every "t." She could not do it better than she has. She's right up there with Nordstrom. I went to college with one of the Nordstroms, and that's who Vickie is. Someone could take what she has done with this business and use it as a business model at Harvard. Nothing is missing. She has everything down, from branding your business to supporting you while you learn and not dropping the ball afterwards. I've reached my professional goal as a CLNC® consultant.

I have gone from reviewing cases to traveling with attorneys across the country, Canada, Mexico and Panama attending depositions, mediations, trials, medical-malpractice conferences, legal seminars and soon to be speaking at my first legal convention.

I hold phone consults on the white sand beaches of Pensacola while watching my son surf. Two days ago, I noticed the bay water in my "backyard" to be perfect glass. I took a break from my cases and went knee boarding with my 11-year-old and his friends. Twelve dolphins joined us and it was one of the best days ever.

> *Vickie gives you all the tools. She's dotted every 'i' and crossed every 't.' She could not do it better than she has.*

> *Becoming a CLNC® consultant has offered me the flexibility to catch the joys of life. Not only am I finally making the money I deserve, my life is everything I've dreamed it to be.*

Becoming a CLNC® consultant has offered me the flexibility to catch the joys of life. Not only am I finally making the money I deserve, my life is everything I've dreamed it to be. I have complete independence and freedom to work when and with whom I wish. Life is amazing! In times of economic uncertainty I have exceeded my income goals each and every year–making four times what I would have as a full-time staff nurse. I am truly blessed and look forward to another fantastic year.

Vickie Propelled Me Past Self-Doubt to CLNC® Success

by Kathy Silay, RN, CLNC, Illinois

> *All through the first case I heard Vickie's words of encouragement in the back of my mind.*

Self-doubt was my biggest obstacle to achieving my dream as a Certified Legal Nurse Consultant^CM. I kept Vickie's brochure on my desk for many years. Periodically, I would take it out and read it again and again. After envisioning what my life could be once I became a CLNC® consultant, self-doubt would set in and I would question my dream. "Where would I find an attorney who actually believes I could help?" At that time I thought attorneys were about the most intimidating breed of professional alive—ranking just above surgeons. I also wondered, "How would I obtain the money to pursue my dream?" I had two small children and worked two jobs.

Then I received a brochure announcing that Vickie's CLNC® 6-Day Certification Seminar would be held in Chicago. I was finally ready to enroll. The week of the seminar was one I will never forget. Again, I had many self-doubts. "Where will I find the time to start my business?" Little did I know, the business would present itself.

My husband and I were redoing our wills and met with our attorney to sign the long-overdue updated versions. Prior to our appointment, I kept

*When
I turned
my report
over to the
attorney, he
was really
impressed.
He asked
if he could
write a
check right
then.*

encouraging my husband to bring some business cards and network with the attorney. Why didn't I consider the same option for myself? I actually ruled out the possibility because I thought this type of attorney couldn't use my CLNC® services. His clients were formulating their wills. How could I possibly assist him? Was I ever wrong.

During our meeting, I rehearsed my elevator speech and thought, "Should I? Shouldn't I? Yes! No! Yes!" Once our business was concluded, I asked the attorney if he might ever need the services of a Certified Legal Nurse Consultant℠. I braced myself for rejection.

He immediately became flustered (I later learned he was actually excited), walked out and returned with a stack of records. Mentioning an upcoming deadline, he asked if I could help him. Once the shock wore off, I calmly answered, "Would you like a verbal or written report?"

All through the first case I heard Vickie's words of encouragement in the back of my mind. When I turned my report over to the attorney, he was really impressed. He asked if he could write a check right then and left the room.

The next thing I heard was a lot of banging and muttering. I thought to myself, "Where does he keep his checkbook?" In actuality, the banging and muttering was him trying to locate all the records for the next case he wanted me to work on.

Thank you, Vickie, and thank you to all the Institute's wonderful CLNC® Mentors.

With Vickie's "Nurses Can Do Anything" Philosophy, I Achieved My CLNC® Dream

by Dawn L. Bruni, RN, MNSc, APN, CLNC, Arkansas

Desiring a career change after 26 years of clinical and educational nursing, I ordered the CLNC® Home-Study Certification Program, completed it in one month and passed the Certification Exam.

Motivated by Vickie's "We are nurses and nurses can do anything!®" philosophy and the inspiring CLNC® Success Stories, I set up my home office, established my fees. Built my website and was ready to start my CLNC® career. I planned to continue my clinical work while I learned the CLNC® business.

I mailed out my first 20 promotional brochures, and three days later I received a call from a highly respected attorney who hired me. My attorney-client was pleased with my work and complimented me for doing a great job.

My biggest suprise came on a break during a deposition. The opposing counsel approached me to ask for my business card to see if I would review a case for him. Since then, I have received dozens of referrals from my attorney-clients. I am amazed how willing attorneys are to refer you to their colleagues when they are pleased with your work.

Thank you, Vickie, for giving me the knowledge, encouragement and confidence to achieve my dream of creating my own successful CLNC® business.

" I mailed out my first 20 promotional brochures, and three days later I received a call from a highly respected attorney who hired me. "

" I am amazed how willing attorneys are to refer you…when they are pleased with your work. "

The Power of Belief— Yes, I Am a Successful CLNC® Consultant!

by Angela Jill (A.J.) Dubs, RN, BSN, CLNC, Kentucky

Wow! I am actually a Certified Legal Nurse Consultant℠ with my own business. I never dreamed it would come together as quickly as Vickie predicted in both her CLNC® Home-Study Certification Program and the CLNC® 6-Day Certification Seminar I attended last fall. Vickie made me promise to continue reading daily for at least 30 days after the seminar, and I was faithful. Now, I am officially my own boss, and I'm on the path to success.

Starting at ground zero in November, I began building my CLNC® business using the powerful formula Vickie taught. I put my vision, core values and mission statement into writing. I delivered my first set of nine marketing packages early in the new year and promptly followed up with the attorneys. Though I was unable to talk with anyone that Friday afternoon, I left several messages.

The next Monday morning, I received a call from the owner of one firm. I was so excited, and at the same time nervous. Later that day, I met with the attorney to discuss his needs and my fees, and to obtain appropriate medical records. Less than three months after starting my business, my CLNC® services had been retained.

This first assignment required many of my new CLNC® skills, but thanks to Vickie's CLNC® Certification Program and the multiple resources it provided, I was ready for the challenges of creating a letter stating my opinion on the deviations from the standards of care and a timeline of the events.

My attorney-client complimented my work product, mentioning the cost-effectiveness and timeliness of my CLNC® services. Finally, he asked me to send him a bill for all charges. "If you're like me," he joked, "when you do a job, you want to be paid for it." He then asked me about meeting on other medical malpractice cases coming up in the near future. I'm blazing the trail now.

Through all the hard work, I heard our "seminar clan" chanting, "We are successful CLNC® consultants!" This was a totally empowering experience for me. Vickie has such a way of motivating you to believe in yourself and your abilities that you *can* do anything.

I continue to use my CLNC® Home-Study Certification Program as a fantastic daily reference. I thank the entire team at Vickie Milazzo Institute for all their encouragement, knowledge and wisdom. The CLNC® 6-Day Certification Seminar was just excellent. I appreciate every staff member's time and effort in quickly responding to my requests for CLNC® mentoring.

Less than three months after starting my business, my CLNC® services had been retained.

Vickie has such a way of motivating you to believe in yourself and your abilities that you can do *anything.*

The possibilities are innumerable, and my potential is infinite.

I feel so lucky to have all the opportunities that are available through this program. The possibilities are innumerable, and my potential is infinite. So many attorneys, so little time. I say, "Go for it. Be the best you can be as a Certified Legal Nurse Consultant^CM!"

Ugly Duckling to Golden Goose— How I Conquered My Fear

by Lawrence H. Frace, RN, CLNC, New Jersey

Two years ago I was a registered nurse with 26 years of experience. I liked my job as a night tour nursing supervisor, but I was suffering from what I call "professional bradycardia." After taking Vickie's CLNC® 6-Day Certification Seminar, I immediately knew my professional (and personal) life was about to change.

I had tried other part-time activities in addition to my full-time nursing career. I was a licensed real estate salesperson, a soil and site evaluator, an Amway distributor and a part-time farmer growing sweet corn on my dad's farm. I even sent away for a program on how to buy real estate with little or no money down. But I finally found my niche as a CLNC® consultant.

Fear Was My Stumbling Block

However, as a new Certified Legal Nurse Consultant℠ I faced a huge stumbling block that initially held me back. I'm sharing my experience so that maybe the obstacle I tripped over time and time again will not be a stumbling block for others. That stumbling block was fear, pure unadulterated fear.

After taking Vickie's CLNC® 6-Day Certification Seminar, I immediately knew my professional (and personal) life was about to change.

I finally found my niche as a Certified Legal Nurse Consultant℠.

I am 6-foot 2-inches tall, two hundred and some-odd pounds, and for the first time I found myself confronting professional fear. So I did what any reasonable and prudent new Certified Legal Nurse Consultant[CM] would do. I procrastinated!

Oh, I dove right in from day one, setting up my office in my basement, complete with used office furniture, a fax machine and multiple phone lines, including an 800 number. I went out and purchased a brand new computer and one of those dot-com address things and posted my website on the Internet, SpectrumMedicalLegal.com. Boy, was I proud of that!

I went through Vickie's *Core Curriculum for Legal Nurse Consulting®* textbook again and again, 30 minutes each day. I subscribed to a host of nursing journals. I started compiling an electronic medical-legal library that I thought was second to none. I went to libraries and book sales and purchased used medical and legal textbooks, carefully displaying them on the walls in my new basement office.

I also created a letter agreement, just like the sample in the *Core Curriculum,* to use for all my anticipated cases. But you know what? I didn't send any of my promotional packets out to attorneys.

Six months later, I said to myself, "But wait a minute. I still have no cases. What's wrong with this picture?" Then it dawned on me: It was fear...fear of actually getting that first case.

I Tried Marketing with My Fingers Crossed

I put my foot down. I finally sent out seven—count them seven—marketing packets. You'll never guess what happened. Two law firms called, and they both wanted to meet with me. Now I thought to myself, "I am in *big* trouble."

I met with attorney #1, and he told me all the real work on the case was done; it just needed to be tabbed and paginated. I walked away from that one and said, "Thank God, at least I didn't get an actual case to work on."

Attorney #2 had told me on the phone that her case involved a person with a physical disability being treated unfairly by an employer. I set up a date to meet with attorney #2 and did what any novice CLNC® consultant would do prior to that all-important first meeting. I researched the disability and how it could be accommodated in the workplace according to cutting-edge, authoritative reports in journals and textbooks. I placed this information in my briefcase and gave it to attorney #2 when I met with her.

She looked through the information and said, "Thank you, this is just what I needed." Then she shook my hand, and that was the end of the meeting.

Now I remember Vickie saying, "Give attorneys what they want and one thing more." The problem was, how did I know, novice that I was, that I'd handed the attorney that "one thing more" up front and thus got no compensation on that case? I chalked my loss up to experience and said once again, "Thank God, at least I didn't get an actual case to work on." I left attorney #2's office empty-handed.

Still having no cases under my CLNC® belt, I started marketing a product to attorneys across the

I met with that attorney, and he gave me the case, the chart, the 'whole enchilada.'... I left with both chart and check in hand.

nation, an idea I had gleaned from Vickie. Several weeks later I started receiving checks in the mail. This was great—go to the mailbox, get the money, send out the product. But now I felt guilty. Here I was, marketing a product to attorneys, and I still did not have a case.

Then I Tried Marketing for Real

I put my foot down again—this time really hard—and sent out seven more marketing packets. Wouldn't you know it, one of the law firms called me. I met with that attorney, and he gave me the case, the chart, the "whole enchilada."

By the way, here's a tip on getting paid by attorneys: Get your money up front. That's Vickie's tip not mine, and it works. When that first attorney-client asked about my fee, I told him what I charged and stated that I get my fee up front. He looked at me, paused, then opened his checkbook and wrote me a check. I left with both chart and check in hand.

Then fear turned into panic as I thought, "Now what am I going to do?" Delving into the chart at home, I created a chronology, got a real feel for the case, took notes and put into practice what I'd learned from Vickie nearly a year-and-a-half earlier. And guess what? Writing the report was fun, which surprised me since I had always thought that would be one of the most difficult tasks.

A month later when I handed the attorney his report, I did include that "one thing more." But this time I got it right, and he was pleased. In fact, he gave me case #2, and without my asking, out came his checkbook. "I know, Larry," he said, "you get your money up front."

"Wow, I sure trained that attorney well," I thought as I left his office with chart and check in hand. Since then, he has given me case #3 and, yes, his checkbook automatically opened up before I left his office.

Your Nursing Skills and Credentials Are for Real

As nurses we often underestimate our abilities, especially if we're doing something new to us, like legal nurse consulting. Don't underestimate your abilities as I did. With your nursing training and experience, coupled with Vickie's knowledge, guidance and CLNC® resources, believe me, you will succeed.

Imagine getting paid for work you absolutely love to do. It's almost like stealing—well, almost. All of Vickie's Certified Legal Nurse Consultants^{CM} have a powerful, marketable product to offer. We all have our CLNC® Certification. Don't ever forget that.

Remember the saying, "You have nothing to fear but fear itself." It took me one-and-a-half years to realize that concept. Don't let that happen to you. Just go out there and "Do It." Do your best and follow Vickie's plan.

Vickie Is for Real

I will close with this true story about Vickie herself. I know it's true because I was there. On day five

All of Vickie's Certified Legal Nurse Consultants^{CM} have a powerful, marketable product... our CLNC® Certification.

> *Thank you,*
> *Vickie...for*
> *'awakening*
> *my potential*
> *and the*
> *nurse*
> *within me.'*

of our CLNC® 6-Day Certification Seminar, our group circulated and signed a thank-you card that read something like this:

> *Dear Vickie, you took all of us Ugly Ducklings and turned us into Golden Geese.*

One student surprised Vickie by presenting the card to her on stage. As Vickie began to read the card, her eyes welled up and for several moments she could not speak. When she did speak, her voice began to quiver—she was visibly moved by that simple card. That's when I knew Vickie truly cares about all her Ducklings and Golden Geese.

Thank you, Vickie, and your fine organization for "awakening my potential and the nurse within me." And thank you, Vickie, for being you.

My CLNC® Success Includes the Freedom to Walk Away at 3:30pm

by Bobbi Black, RN, CLNC, Iowa

After working in a large clinic for 22 years, I retired. I was 48, my life was changing, my workplace was changing and I qualified for early retirement, so I took it. My family was growing up, and I began to wonder, "What am I going to do now?" Then I found Vickie Milazzo Institute's LegalNurse.com website and became intrigued. I knew I had the experience as a nurse to become a Certified Legal Nurse Consultant^{CM}–I decided to take the CLNC® 6-Day Certification Seminar. Vickie's CLNC® Certification Program is the key to my CLNC® success.

Becoming a Certified Legal Nurse Consultant^{CM} has such a positive impact on my life. It spells freedom–more financial freedom, being able to work from home doing what I love to do any time I want, but also being able to walk away from it at 3:30 in the afternoon. I'm free to walk downstairs to find my husband in his office–he also works from home. We are then free to choose what we want to do with the rest of our day.

When asked by other nurses if a career in legal nurse consulting can be successful, I repeat what Vickie told me, "Absolutely, if you're passionate about it."

Market, market, market, even when you're busy. Anywhere I market my CLNC® business, I show up

Anywhere I market my CLNC® business, I show up with independence and confidence.

My nursing experience and Vickie's CLNC® Certification Program were the biggest factors in winning the case.

with independence and confidence, just like Vickie taught me. I walk in the door and say, "Here I am. I can help you."

My CLNC® business really took off when I located a group of attorneys and camped out on their door step. Today those attorneys are some of my best clients. One of the attorneys recently told me, "The reason I hired you is because I was tired of stepping over you when I came through the door in the morning." We laugh about it now, but my persistence paid off.

In Vickie's CLNC® 6-Day Certification Program, she encourages her students to send out a newsletter to attorney-prospects and clients. My newsletter helps me connect with attorneys and I can count on receiving numerous phone calls each time I send one.

My CLNC® consulting work is always interesting. Many RNs think legal nurse consultants consult only on medical malpractice or personal injury cases. Some of my favorite cases are the ones that I wouldn't think I'd be involved in, like a murder trial or a legal malpractice case involving a will.

The case outcomes can also be exciting. My first big attorney-client asked me to review a medical malpractice case for merit. I found a gross deviation in the standards of care and located an expert for the attorney. That case went to mediation and settled for a larger amount than anyone expected.

While that litigation was in progress, my attorney-client asked me to begin work on another case.

A doctor had previously reviewed the case's medical records, but when the attorney asked for my help, I discovered numerous things the doctor had overlooked. Then, right before the case went to trial, the attorney asked me to accompany him to court. When the defense expert denied the validity of a particular radiology report, I whispered to my attorney-client, "Trust me on this–show him this report." The second report invalidated the medical expert for the defense and upended their case. My nursing experience and Vickie's CLNC® Certification Program were the biggest factors in winning the case.

A large part of my CLNC® consulting success is due to Vickie's enthusiasm and her encouraging words, such as We Are Nurses and We Can Do Anything!®

Vickie's CLNC® Mentoring Program is another part of my CLNC® consulting success. I enjoy working through the problems I encounter. I contact the CLNC® Mentors any time I'm stymied. It's reassuring to brainstorm with these CLNC® Pros.

What makes my CLNC® business successful? By thinking outside the box, using my nursing skills and remembering Vickie's CLNC® training, I successfully evaluate cases and help my attorney-clients gain the best outcomes. I'm so excited about my CLNC® career. I'm living my dream of being a successful CLNC® consultant, having a great time and being rewarded financially for the work I do!

> *I'm living my dream of being a successful CLNC® consultant, having a great time and being rewarded financially for the work I do!*

I Accomplished My One-Year Goal in One Day of Exhibiting

by Tina J. Little, RN, BS, MBA, CLNC, Illinois

The Monday after I came home from the CLNC® 6-Day Certification Seminar, Vickie's voice was in my head saying, "Today's the best day to begin." Right away I started setting my marketing goals.

During my first year as a Certified Legal Nurse Consultant^CM, I wanted at least five cases. I wrote that down in my marketing plan. Then I read Vickie's book, *Flash 55 Promotions: 55 FREE Ways to Promote Your CLNC® Business,* from cover to cover. Using her pointers, I set up my website, created my promotional package and mailed out my packets.

I discovered that a local trial lawyers' association was having a conference. I wrote to ask if I could exhibit. That was scary, but I put myself out there, hearing Vickie's voice again, telling me that a CLNC® consultant is an attorney's "secret weapon."

At the lawyers' conference, I approached attorneys and talked about my specialty, trauma. I'm an ER nurse, plus I have 27 years as a paramedic. That combination of experience gives me a unique insight. As it turned out, I met an attorney who had come to the conference looking specifically for a CLNC® consultant with a background in emergency medical services and trauma. I left the conference with six cases.

My first case was exciting because it called on all my trauma background. A man developed chest pains at a ball game. The EMS team walked him down two flights of steps, and when he got to the bottom, he went into cardiac arrest. Although I started my CLNC® business hoping I could work on the defense side, advocating for nurses and other healthcare practitioners, I understand that mistakes are sometimes made. That was the situation here. The patient died due to overexertion of the heart. Using my nursing and paramedic background along with my CLNC® training, I helped the attorney build his case.

Becoming a CLNC® Consultant Changed My World

Being a CLNC® consultant has changed my emotional, mental, physical and spiritual world. I care more about who I am, and every day I believe more in what I can do for my attorney-clients and their clients. I feel I have so much to give to this profession. And I'm doing what I love.

I set my own schedule. Being my own boss is incredibly affirming. As nurses, we take what's available. As a CLNC® consultant, I control which cases I choose to work on and who I choose to work for. My CLNC® income in the six months since I became certified has been amazing.

One attorney did tell me I charge too much. I said, "I hope you find somebody to help you, but

I'm doing what I love.

My CLNC® income in the six months since I became certified has been amazing.

*I help
attorneys
win cases.
And
Vickie was
right—
I'm their
secret
weapon.*

she won't be as worthy as I am." He chuckled. About two weeks later, he called back and asked if I would work on his case—for my usual fee of course.

Sometimes I'm still scared, but I keep putting myself out there, taking risks and telling myself I can do this. I help attorneys win cases. And Vickie was right—I'm their secret weapon.

Vickie Gave Me the Confidence to Forge My New CLNC® Career

by Bridget D. King, RN, BSN, RNFA, CNOR, CLNC, California

As a nurse for more than 20 years, my experience includes OR, ICU and home health. Because of a recent life change, it was time for my career to change too. A friend recommended that I try Vickie's CLNC® Certification Program. I purchased and completed the home-study version. Excited about the possibilities, I also attended the CLNC® 6-Day Certification Seminar.

I left the seminar ready, willing and able to forge my exciting new career as a Certified Legal Nurse Consultant℠. Vickie taught us so much valuable information about starting a business. She taught us how important it was to get out there and market our services.

Vickie's CLNC® Certification Program gave me the confidence to start my own practice. I began advertising my CLNC® services on a website for trial lawyers. Boom—my consulting practice started! Now, most of my business comes from word-of-mouth referrals. The majority of my cases are for personal injury attorneys.

"Vickie's CLNC® Certification Program gave me the confidence to start my own practice."

Vickie is a wonderful person. I can't say enough about her or her CLNC® Certification Program. I continually reread the material.

My goal is to quit the hospital and practice full-time as a Certified Legal Nurse Consultant^CM. I will reach my goal!

Vickie is a wonderful person. I can't say enough about her or her CLNC® Certification Program.

Shocked to Success with Vital Signs Still Intact

by Arlene Santiago-Tribbett,
RN, BSN, CLNC, New Jersey

For the past eight years, I've been a home-care and ER/trauma nurse. My nursing career had become unsatisfying, so I began searching in a new career direction. I thought about graduate school, but none of the programs seemed worthy of my time or money. Before becoming a nurse, I was a police officer, and the law always fascinated me. When I saw an ad for Vickie's CLNC® Certification Program in a nursing magazine, I researched the field and signed up for the Institute's program.

The CLNC® 6-Day Certification Seminar impressed me from the first day. Vickie gave away information so freely, and I experienced nurses from all over the country coming together in unity and fully supportive of each other. The seminar was so motivating that I regained the pride I once had for nursing. Vickie and her CLNC® Certification Program did that for me.

The week after the seminar was like a dream. I had an appointment to see an attorney for personal reasons. I told him I was a Certified Legal Nurse Consultant℠ and mentioned the services I provided. He stopped me in mid-sentence and called his associates into his office to hear what I had to say. "Where have you been?" he asked and explained

Vickie gave away information so freely... The seminar was so motivating that I regained the pride I once had for nursing.

That one week with Vickie was the most challenging, yet the most exciting of my life.

that his firm desperately needed a qualified CLNC® consultant.

I told him I charged $125/hr and needed a 50% retainer, and he gave me three cases with the promise of two more. He went on to say that he would introduce me to other attorneys who could use my CLNC® services.

I am still in shock. I never expected any of this. That one week with Vickie was the most challenging, yet the most exciting of my life. Now, I actually have work in my hands. My life is headed in a new, exciting and profitable direction I never could have imagined before I attended Vickie's CLNC® 6-Day Certification Seminar.

I Am All That I Can Be as a Successful Certified Legal Nurse Consultant^{CM}

by Teresa C. Vitale, RN, CCM, CLNC, California

I attended the CLNC® 6-Day Certification Seminar to learn about legal nurse consulting and prepare for the future. I had been the director of nursing in a 176-bed facility, a certified case manager and a nursing supervisor. While I enjoyed the daily challenges, I also dreaded the burnout I knew would come.

The CLNC® Certification Program gave me the opportunity to step out of my comfort zone, my "little box," and gain a new perspective on my career. I met brilliant nurses from all over the United States and found that we shared a bond. We were all so different in many ways and yet so similar. We were there because we were not afraid to explore the challenge of being all that we could be.

I returned to my position feeling more informed and prepared, even empowered to deal with my profession's everyday challenges. I also felt an obligation to educate my staff and friends. Vickie planted seeds of ideas that had a tremendous impact on my daily activities.

Shortly after I returned, I was deposed about quality of care issues for a case. I was impressed by

"Vickie planted seeds of ideas that had a tremendous impact on my daily activities."

"I have more energy and quality time to spend with my family."

the professionalism and kindness the defense attorneys showed me. I casually mentioned attending the CLNC® 6-Day Certification Seminar.

After interviewing with the law partners, I gave my former employer a month's notice as a professional courtesy. I took a brief vacation and prepared to launch my new career as a CLNC® consultant. In other words, I went shopping for a new wardrobe.

I now work with a staff of brilliant young professionals. There is a mutual respect and admiration for the contributions each brings to the firm. My added bonus is that I have more energy and quality time to spend with my family.

Achieving the CLNC® Certification motivated and energized me to step out of my comfort zone and explore ways to be all that I could be. Vickie's training provided me with the basic ingredients necessary to be successful. I tell all who will listen that the learning process only stops when you are dead. The skills and ideas presented in the CLNC® Certification Program gave me a whole new perspective on my own self-worth.

Vickie's CLNC® Certification Gives Hope and Confidence

by Heidi Santiago, RN, CLNC, New York

So many of the seminars I have been to as a nurse have not lived up to what they say. Vickie's CLNC® 6-Day Certification Seminar certainly proved to be different for me.

I drove home from the seminar to my son's football game that night and immediately applied Vickie's 3-foot rule. I started talking to the gentleman next to me whose son was also in the game. When I mentioned that I just returned home from a seminar, he asked, "What kind of seminar?" I replied, "Legal nurse consulting." We began to talk. He said he was a medical malpractice attorney from a large firm and had a case he wanted me to review. He also said he had heard about Vickie and the Institute.

That same weekend at a wine and cheese party, my brother introduced me to a personal injury attorney. When I asked him to get me into his firm to meet the other attorneys, he said, "Sure." I networked just like Vickie taught us, and in only one weekend I got one case and an introduction that will put me in touch with other potential attorney-clients.

The most beneficial part of Vickie's CLNC® 6-Day Certification Seminar was the amount of confidence she imparted to us all. Now, I can walk into any attorney's office with the confidence of success, knowing legal terminology, knowing the

> *"I networked just like Vickie taught us, and in only one weekend I got one case and an introduction that will put me in touch with other potential attorney-clients."*

services I can provide, and knowing that attorneys will pay for my nursing knowledge and experience.

I walked away from Vickie's CLNC® 6-Day Certification Seminar with hope. Vickie taught us to never devalue our nursing knowledge but to put a top-dollar price on it. I thought I was crazy to start my own business now, at age 40 with 12 years in home health nursing. I've tried so many home-based businesses, from network marketing to mail order, that never ever panned out. Vickie's program taught me how to succeed in a business that has already started to provide an exceptional living for me and my family.

Vickie's program taught me how to succeed in a business that has already started to provide an exceptional living for me and my family.

Take the
Fast Track
to Financial
Freedom

How I Matched My Hospital Salary in 5 Months as a Part-Time Certified Legal Nurse Consultant^{CM}

by George H. Cox, RN, BSN, MS, CRNA, CLNC, Nevada

I wanted new challenges and more excitement in my all-too-routine professional life.

After 26 years in critical care nursing including 16 years as a certified registered nurse anesthetist (CRNA), I had become restless again. My CRNA practice provided me with professional recognition, respect within the community and the economic security of a six-digit income. Still, I was not happy. I wanted new challenges and more excitement in my all-too-routine professional life. I had often thought about attending law school. Realistically, however, at the age of 51 and with two children soon heading off to college, a complete career change was not an option.

For years I had seen ads for Vickie Milazzo Institute's CLNC® Certification Program in various nursing publications, but I did not know what a Certified Legal Nurse Consultant^CM did. One day I came across the Institute's ad again. This time I called and asked to speak with a CLNC® Mentor. My call was promptly returned and my many questions were answered. The most remarkable thing about that 30-minute conversation was the sincerity and genuine enthusiasm of the CLNC® Mentor. This turned out to be one of the most significant phone calls of my life. Immediately, I enrolled in the CLNC® 6-Day Certification Seminar.

The seminar was simply fascinating. Beyond the wealth of information and the quality of the instruction, I was completely enthralled. I found the class atmosphere exciting and inspiring. I studied each evening, not because I had to, but because I wanted to. It had been a long time since something had aroused my interest like the idea of practicing as a Certified Legal Nurse Consultant^CM.

Vickie's Warmth and Encouragement Sparked My Determination

After the CLNC® Certification Exam on day six, I ran into Vickie in the hall. I told her how much I had enjoyed the seminar and how determined I was to make the knowledge I had gained work for me. She hugged me, thanked me and told me she was looking forward to someday reading my CLNC® Success Story. From that moment on, I became determined to pursue my CLNC® practice until I had a success story I could proudly send to Vickie.

During the next four weeks, I studied Vickie's advanced resources. I took notes and created a reference binder. I had faith in my ability to succeed. I had a burning desire to make it work. I hoped I had the courage and persistence to see it through.

Because I already possessed specialized training, knowledge and experience in critical care nursing and anesthesia nursing, I decided to emphasize anesthesiology, operating room, post anesthesia recovery, critical care and emergency care in my Certified Legal Nurse Consultant^{CM} practice. While I recognized this choice could limit my opportunities, I felt most familiar and confident in these clinical areas. I also set my fees higher than the national average because I believed my specialties could command higher rates. With my busy anesthesia practice limiting my availability for appointments with local attorneys, I decided to also market to established CLNC® colleagues who might need my specialized knowledge.

With those decisions made, Southern Nevada Professional Legal Nurse Consultants was born. I mailed out dozens of introductory letters and brochures to law firms and legal nurse consulting firms nationwide. I also used my current anesthesia practice as a

> *The seminar was simply fascinating. Beyond the wealth of information and the quality of the instruction, I was completely enthralled.*

stepping-stone, networking for my CLNC® business at every appropriate opportunity.

With this strategy, my first attorney-client became my easiest to secure. That one contact has since blossomed into others. Attorneys really do talk to each other.

I Equaled My Top CRNA Income in Just 5 Months as a CLNC® Consultant

Five months after completing the CLNC® Certification Program, I had achieved the following:

- Consulted with an East Coast plaintiff attorney on a case involving an anesthesiologist.
- Consulted on a case involving a CRNA for a defense attorney on the West Coast.
- Provided expert opinion in a case involving a CRNA for a government healthcare facility in the Midwest.
- Reviewed a number of records closer to home for both plaintiff and defense attorneys.
- Performed subcontracting work for other Certified Legal Nurse Consultants^{CM}.

By far, the most interesting and personally rewarding case I have been involved in was a medical records review in which I identified tampering with the record.

The best part is I have more work than I could ever have imagined finding so quickly. In order to devote more time to my CLNC® practice, I recently resigned from an administrative nursing position I had held for years.

Based on a 12-month period, my earnings as a CLNC® consultant closely approximate my established earnings as a very well-paid CRNA. Could I give up my anesthesia practice and earn the same amount as a full-time CLNC® consultant? Yes, I could, perhaps even significantly more. But right now, I want to continue practicing as a CRNA. I enjoy anesthesia nursing and the patients it brings me into contact with each day. Sometime in the future, I will end my anesthesia practice and become a full-time Certified Legal Nurse Consultant℠. For now, it is just nice to know I have that option.

That is what becoming a CLNC® consultant has given me: options. Although I'm extremely busy balancing two careers, I am investing the additional time not because I have to, but because the work is fun. Professionally, I am enjoying my activities more than I ever have. I often think to myself, "They call this work?" I love the challenge. I love the "investigative detective" work. I love the professional recognition for a job well done.

So Vickie, this is the CLNC® Success Story you said you'd be looking for. I don't think either of us thought it would happen so fast. For that, I have one special person to thank: Thank you, Vickie!

> *My earnings as a CLNC® consultant closely approximate my established earnings as a very well-paid CRNA.*

> *I often think to myself, 'They call this work?'... I love the professional recognition for a job well done.*

I Am Living My Passion Making $175,000 This Year

by Sheila Silvus Chesanow, RN, MS, CLNC, Tennessee

> "This year I will make about $175,000."

> "The benefits of being a Certified Legal Nurse Consultant are endless. I enjoy staying at home."

After I became a Certified Legal Nurse Consultant^CM, I worked for a corporation doing internal auditing. After two years, a CLNC® friend told me about an opportunity to have an exclusive Certified Legal Nurse Consultant contract with an attorney. At first I wasn't sure I wanted an exclusive contract with any attorney because I did not know if he would have enough work for me. I was wrong. I ended up signing a contract with this attorney-client for $150,000 annually for 40 hours a week. This year I will make about $175,000.

Technology has been a big plus for my CLNC® business. My husband retired and we moved to Tennessee. My attorney-client lives in California. Technology allows me to work full time at home out of an office that used to be part of our barn as I watch over llamas grazing outside. My attorney-client, who has a protected server that allows her to download documents, copies everything to a disk. One of the best things I've adopted from one of Tom's Tech Tips was dual monitors. I review the files from my attorney-client on one screen while I write my report using the second screen. I also take my work on the road when I travel. My husband races cars so I can just pack up my bag with my laptop and go with him. It's great because my legal nurse consulting business is completely portable.

The benefits of being a Certified Legal Nurse Consultant^CM are endless. I work out every morning, have coffee with friends, then I go to work. The more I work, the more money I make. I can work 50 hours one week and take a day off the next whenever I choose. In my prior job, I only slept in my own bed about eight nights a month because I had to travel so much. Now as a Certified Legal Nurse Consultant^CM, I enjoy staying at home.

When I worked at a full-time job, I could count my friends on one hand. Now, I am more involved in my community and I'm active in the charities that are important to me.

I was going to semi-retire, do a little CLNC® work but not really do much. However, I have stayed busy and have had numerous offers for additional legal nurse consulting work. When this happens, I contact my network of CLNC® peers. The *NACLNC®* Directory has a wealth of CLNC® consultants who I can refer business to or recommend as experts.

My advice to nurses is to stop waiting—do it now. Become a Certified Legal Nurse Consultant^CM today. Stop procrastinating!

The NACLNC® Directory has a wealth of CLNC® consultants who I can refer business to or recommend as experts.

My advice to nurses is to stop waiting— do it now.

The company president... had the foresight to recognize how valuable I could be as a Certified Legal Nurse Consultant^{CM}.

I Earned $125,000 in 4 Months as a CLNC® Consultant

by Darlene Bellows, RN, CLNC, Tennessee

I was the director of nursing at a nursing home when I decided to become a Certified Legal Nurse Consultant^{CM}. One day, a staff nurse told me she was taking the CLNC® Home-Study Certification Program. She shared some of the information with me, and it piqued my interest.

A year later, I left the director of nursing position and accepted a position in the legal department of a long term care company. I began reviewing medical records involved in litigation for the in-house attorney. Then the company hired a new president who began an initiative to reduce the number of lawsuits. He had the foresight to recognize how valuable I could be as a Certified Legal Nurse Consultant^{CM}. The company paid for me to take the CLNC® 6-Day Certification Seminar in May.

Thrilled and excited, I headed for Orlando to become a Certified Legal Nurse Consultant^{CM}. I never thought I'd make it through that week. There was so much information and so many new things to learn. But with Vickie constantly reminding us that we were successful CLNC® consultants, I passed the test.

I took my new knowledge back to work and continued assisting the company in defending against lawsuits. I was promoted to director of the department, hired another nurse and sent her to the CLNC® 6-Day Certification Seminar in October.

I Accepted My Husband's Outrageous Holiday Challenge

I soon realized I was doing the job of a legal nurse consultant and getting paid $35/hr instead of the $100-$150/hr I could be making on my own. When I complained about this to my husband, he said, "Why don't you try it part time and see if you like it?"

That was in early December. With the holidays looming, our son's wedding scheduled for two days after Christmas and a houseful of guests expected for both events, I said, "Maybe after the first of the year."

My husband quickly came back with, "What are you waiting for?" I always accept a challenge, especially from my husband. He has steered me in the right direction for the last 20 years.

The next day I called a defense attorney who handled some of my company's cases in Florida. I asked if he thought I could succeed at legal nurse consulting. He said I would be great, and he would keep me busy full time. I told him to send me just one case for now and tell me how I did.

The following week, just days before Christmas (and the wedding), the attorney sent me the medi-

I called a defense attorney... He said I would be great, and he would keep me busy full time.

cal records. Not a large case, but big enough for my
first one. He asked if I could report back to him by
New Year's Day. Once again I was challenged, and
I rose to the occasion and got the assignment done
in plenty of time. The feedback I received was that
my work was exactly what he needed.

My Part-Time CLNC® Career Blossomed into Full-Time Success

From that point, I continued to work at my full-
time job, then come home every night and work
several hours on my new part-time job, as well as
up to ten hours on the weekends. No one at my
full-time job knew I was moonlighting, but they
wondered why all of a sudden I only worked eight
hours instead of my usual 12-14-hour days.

Within three months my legal nurse consulting
cases were piling up so much that I had to seek help
from a CLNC® subcontractor. I heard another nurse
in the office complaining that she could earn much
more as a Certified Legal Nurse Consultant^CM and
really wanted to pursue it. I recruited her as a subcontractor. Together, we continued turning out the
work for another few months.

After attending my first *National Alliance of Certified Legal Nurse Consultants (NACLNC®)* Annual
Conference in March, I went home and told my
husband my goal was to be on my own no later
than the end of the year. Two events soon sped up
the process. First, my part-time CLNC® career was
generating enough work that I had to hire another
subcontractor. My goal was and still is to produce

top quality work and get it back to the attorney-client in a timely manner. Second, management changed the direction of our department at my full-time job. This made it easy for me to decide to jump in with both feet and go full time as a CLNC® consultant.

The decision was still scary. All I could think was, "What if I don't get any more cases? Good thing my husband loves peanut-butter-and-jelly sandwiches and I diet most of the time."

Nevertheless, I made the plunge in May. For a short while, I could not keep up with the records. I sent my marketing packet to every defense attorney I had come to know through my former company. I also phoned these attorneys to let them know where I was and what I was doing. As a result, within four months as a full-time independent CLNC® consultant, I billed more than $125,000.

Currently, I consult for four nursing home defense attorneys. They keep my business growing. I organize and review medical records; prepare brief or detailed chronologies and narrative summaries; do research and phone consultation; and help long term care companies assess their medical records for liability exposure and documentation accuracy.

One case makes me especially proud—analyzing four years of one patient's nursing home records. The assignment took me 89 hours. When I asked my attorney-client for feedback, he said, "You certainly are detailed. I'll call back when I get through it." Two weeks later he phoned to say my chronology was the best work he had ever seen. Everything

Within four months as a full-time independent CLNC® consultant, I billed more than $125,000.

He phoned to say my chronology was the best work he had ever seen. Everything he needed from the record was in my CLNC® report.

he needed from the record was in my CLNC® report, and he would be able to use it instead of hauling the volumes of medical records to depositions and mediations. He appreciated how thorough I had been.

Learning to Break the 8-5 Habit Was Part of the Fun

After years of working an 8-5 job, it was hard for me to break the habit. It took me about three months to realize I did not have to feel guilty if I went for a walk with my 84-year-old dad, had lunch with friends, took a day off to pamper myself or spent time with my grandchildren. My best friend and I took our first "girl trip" together to Florida. Of course, I had my laptop, medical records and marketing brochures with me, and I had appointments to see some attorneys.

The money is great. My CLNC® business continues to be very successful. I've had up to 20 cases in progress at one time and as many as five subcontractors working with me. Last year I billed $330,000. But the greatest satisfaction comes when an attorney calls or emails to say, "Your work was awesome. It will be a great help to me in depositions, mediations and at trial."

My success has allowed my husband to retire and help me in my business. In the past couple of years we have taken three fabulous vacations. I've also had time to spend with my three wonderful grandchildren and with other Certified Legal Nurse Consultants[CM].

I attribute my CLNC® success to several things: my many years of nursing experience; my experience in the risk management and legal departments in long term care; my supportive family and friends who encouraged me to take a leap of faith; and the foresight of the company president who sent me to the CLNC® 6-Day Certification Seminar. Vickie's CLNC® Certification Program was great, informative and certainly the beginning of my success.

In the past couple of years we have taken three fabulous vacations. I've also had time to spend with my three wonderful grandchildren.

My $100,000 Tax Return Put Me Over the Moon with Joy

by Sharon Miller, RN, BSN, CLNC, Maryland

Hi Vickie, I just had to tell you the great news. I just finished my taxes and I am happy, no make that thrilled, no make that "over the moon with joy" to tell you that I earned more than $100,000.00. I went ahead and incorporated and named my CLNC® business when the work started coming in faster than I could keep up. I just keep working hard trying to keep up with all of the work and make sure that I still put out top-quality work product. I was so happy when one of my attorney-clients forwarded my information to another law firm. I did a case for them and they were so happy with the "excellent CLNC® work product" that I provided that they immediately forwarded another case to me.

I have been keeping so busy and I absolutely love being able to work for myself. I still have the law firm that I first started working for. I have also gotten cases from the medical-malpractice attorneys, nursing home negligence and more. I am keeping so busy that I am going to have to start hiring CLNC® subcontractors. Luckily I met this incredible nurse and I convinced her to go through your CLNC® Certification Program, which she just recently completed. Now that she is a CLNC® consultant, I am ready to ask her to subcontract with me on my huge case load.

I now have cases going to trial. I am working with three attorney-clients who are in the first round of trials and two attorney-clients in the second group of trials. These cases all need detailed chronological summaries–something that I have been providing to these law firms for deposition preps.

Anyway, I just thought I would let you know how happy I am that I became a Certified Legal Nurse Consultant^{CM}. I love the way that I can combine my love and knowledge of nursing with my love of law. Thank you, Vickie, a hundred times over for helping me become a successful Certified Legal Nurse Consultant^{CM}. You rock!

I hope my positive experiences will help other Certified Legal Nurse Consultants^{CM} go for that BIG success. I feel honored to share my CLNC® successes.

> *I am keeping so busy that I am going to have to start hiring CLNC® subcontractors.*

My CLNC® Business Is the Ticket to Retiring in 5 Years

by Carol Riley, RN, MHA, CNAA, HFA, CLNC, Indiana

After five years as a Certified Legal Nurse Consultant[CM], my success was moderate, and I was staying busy part time. I had not been overly aggressive with marketing and had settled into the security of receiving cases from my regular attorney-clients on a "trickle in, trickle out" basis. I was enjoying the time to pursue my hobbies while still contributing to the family income and paying for my daughter's college tuition. Jordanne is in nursing school, and I felt good knowing my earnings would help place another nurse in the ranks by the time I was ready to retire.

You Never Know Where Your Next Referral Will Come From

Little did I know that my daughter would provide my best referral. Remember how Vickie tells us to market ourselves to anyone and everyone? As my story proves, you never know where your next referral will come from.

About a year ago Jordanne was at her part-time job in a local chain restaurant. One Friday night a nice looking young man wearing National Guard fatigues pulled up in a Jaguar. As his order arrived and she checked him out, she admired his Jaguar and commented that the National Guard must be doing well for him. At that he smiled and told her his real job was as a med-mal defense attorney. She nonchalantly replied, "My mother works with attorneys."

He asked what I did. When she told him I was a Certified Legal Nurse Consultant[CM], he almost dropped his food. He immediately started asking what kind of cases I specialized in and whether I had room in my caseload for more. He dug around but couldn't find a business card.

Fortunately, Jordanne had one of my cards in her wallet and gave it to him. He literally took a napkin, wrote down his personal email address, business and cell phone numbers, and asked her to have me call him ASAP. He had cases to send me.

She couldn't wait to get home and tell me about the encounter. It's been a long time since anyone wrote their number on a napkin for me!

Letters of Recommendation Are My Best Marketing Tool

The next evening I called him on his cell phone. It sounded like he was at a party, but he took the time to ask about my clinical experience, my legal nurse consulting experience and my availability. I learned he was with a big firm in a major city downstate.

On Monday, I sent him my brochure, resume, letter of recommendation and work product samples.

> *He and his paralegal had just sorted through a 'tabletop full of cases' to decide which ones they would send me.*

By Thursday, I hadn't heard from him. On Friday, I nervously made that follow-up call Vickie stresses as essential to our success.

He answered his business phone himself. When I asked if he had any questions, he said he didn't. My heart sank. *Then* he added that he and his paralegal had just sorted through a "tabletop full of cases" to decide which ones they would send me.

I asked if he wanted to know what I charged, and he said, "Sure, but it doesn't matter. That letter of recommendation convinced me you have exactly the skills we need." He was referring to the letter from one of my attorney-clients, a well-known plaintiff attorney.

As Vickie says, a good letter of recommendation is one of your best marketing tools. This new defense attorney-client said he would make sure he didn't have to try any cases against "your plaintiff attorney" because he didn't want to go up against me as the opposing expert. I nearly fell out of my chair.

I'm Now on Track for Retirement—or a Jaguar

The cases started arriving the following week and the flood hasn't stopped. After receiving the first case, I emailed to advise him that I was available and to inform him of my hourly rate. He immediately offered an additional 33% if I could complete the case in two weeks. Needless to say, I met that deadline and enjoyed the premium. Since then I've been so busy I've had to use CLNC® subcontractors.

I can't believe my good fortune. My husband is astounded that my "little business" is making so much money. I just paid off my Jeep and bought a new quilting machine so I can enjoy my hobby in my spare time—even though I don't have as much spare time since my Certified Legal Nurse Consultant[CM] practice took off. Oh well, the quilting machine will be there for my "real" retirement.

My goal is to retire in five years. With Vickie's advice and training, my CLNC® business is sure to make that retirement happen on schedule, leaving me professionally fulfilled and financially secure. You never know, I just might trade that Jeep for a Jag.

My goal is to retire in five years. With Vickie's advice and training, my CLNC® business is sure to make that retirement happen on schedule.

How I Achieved Big City Success in a Small Town

by Danita F. Deaton, RN, BA, CLNC, Texas

Most people think of my small town in Texas as just a blip on the map as they drive through to the Louisiana casinos. But I chose to settle here. Born in Sulphur, Louisiana, I grew up in Alaska, where I was a CPA for ten years, got my nursing degree in Denver and then moved to Southeast Texas.

I went directly into adult intensive care. I've worked in numerous areas of nursing, including ER and management. I was director of nursing in a long term, extended care unit and I've done a lot of quality assurance, so I have a broad background in nursing and administration.

As nurses, we're here to do a job, and I think we should do it well, but the medical field has a lot of problems. I'm a patient advocate, and I knew there had to be a better way to help. I had seen information about the Institute's CLNC® 6-Day Certification Seminar, and I had looked up Vickie Milazzo Institute on the Internet. I began thinking legal nurse consulting might be the road I was searching for. I contacted the Institute and received a packet, but I didn't follow through. I'm a world-class procrastinator.

Then I took a position as director of a neonatal intensive care unit. Because of my critical care background, my employer also talked me into being director of the telemetry department. Instead of wearing a pager 24/7, I was basically on call 48/14 in two different units. I finally left this extremely stressful job for PRN work in Houston.

In the meantime, I had remarried. I wanted to spend more time with my husband and my two-year-old grandson. I was dissatisfied with where nursing was going for me. I knew I had more to offer, and I didn't want to retire with a bad back. So I checked out Amway and Mary Kay and took a learn-at-home course in real estate.

I Decided Enough Was Enough

One day my daughter, who worked at a car wash, met an attorney bringing his Jaguar to be cleaned. She told him, "My mom's a nurse. She could help you with some cases."

The next thing I knew, this attorney phoned, asking me to review a couple of nursing home cases. I put in four hours at most on each of those cases. That felt great—I could do this. Yet despite follow-up, that attorney didn't call me back.

I decided enough was enough. I wasn't getting any younger, and I didn't want to work nights anymore. I found that packet from Vickie Milazzo Institute, read it through, decided I was going to do this and signed up for the VIP CLNC® Success System.

I decided I was going to do this and signed up for the VIP CLNC® Success System.

At the CLNC® 6-Day Certification Seminar, I felt like a few hundred light bulbs went off in my head.

> *After the seminar I was so fired up, I decided to follow Vickie's advice and do something toward my new career every day.*

> *The next day I telephoned that attorney, met with him and took home a case.*

Vickie Inspired Me to Go for It

At the CLNC® 6-Day Certification Seminar, I felt like a few hundred light bulbs went off in my head. I realized I hadn't done a fourth of what I could have done to help that attorney on those first two cases, and the money I received was nothing compared to what I could make. This was wonderful.

After the seminar I was so fired up, I decided to follow Vickie's advice and do something toward my new career every day. I spread out all of the materials from my VIP CLNC® Success System and marked my calendar. I worked out a budget. I hired a CPA and an attorney to incorporate my company. Both my CPA and my attorney gave me some referrals. I wrote the names in my *I Am a Successful CLNC® Success Journal.* Three weeks after receiving my CLNC® Certification, I was in business.

I kept looking at that *Success Journal,* at the quotes on each page. I knew I was going to do this, but besides being a procrastinator, I'm also a perfectionist. I didn't want to call those referrals until I had everything perfect. Finally, my attorney phoned and said, "Danita, you haven't called this guy yet. I told him to expect your call. He's waiting."

The CLNC® Mentors Guided Me to Success

The next day I telephoned that attorney, met with him and took home a case. At first I just stared at the file. I didn't even have my intro letter written, yet I had a case. Easy to say I could do it, easy to fake it while I was in the attorney's office, but now I had to deliver on my promise. I remembered those two early cases and never hearing back from the attorney. I couldn't let that happen again.

This time I had Vickie's VIP CLNC® Success System materials and unlimited CLNC® Mentoring. I called the Institute and described the case.

The CLNC® Mentor said, "First, take a few deep breaths." After talking with her and with the attorney again, I wrote a 30-page report advising the attorney that the case was meritorious.

Meanwhile, I wrote my intro letter. Again, I called the Institute for help, and I put together a simple package with my resume, sample reports and a bulleted list of ten CLNC® services. A month after attending the CLNC® 6-Day Certification Seminar, I mailed out my first six marketing packets.

The next week I was ready to send out six more packets, as Vickie encouraged us to do. Before I could leave to go to the post office, a paralegal from one of the big malpractice firms called. Two of their attorneys wanted to see me. I didn't want to say I was available anytime, and I was still working two nights a week, so I scheduled the interview on a day when I wouldn't be trying to sleep.

I walked into my interview wearing my nice black suit. Both attorneys had my packet on the table in front of them. When I asked why they called me, one attorney said, "We were impressed with your marketing package. It was very profes-

I mailed out my first six packets.... One of the big malpractice firms called. Two of their attorneys wanted to see me.

sional, with no grammatical errors, no misspellings." My package showed I had taken the time to do it right.

Vickie Helped Me Anticipate Every Question

In my briefcase I had the list of questions and answers Vickie had told us to expect in interviews. The attorneys' questions matched that list almost verbatim.

One of their biggest questions concerned my rates. When I said I charged $125.00 an hour, the first attorney said, "That's kind of high, don't you think?" I kept quiet, almost sitting on my hands, as Vickie advised.

After a few seconds, he said, "Tell me why I should pay you $125.00 an hour."

"Because I'm good at what I do," I said. When he asked what was the difference between me and a paralegal, I said, "Being a paralegal would be a step backward. I have an expertise, paralegals have an expertise and you have an expertise. I'm not an attorney, and you're not a nurse. That's why we can work together."

When we finished the interview, one attorney asked if I wanted to work for them full time. I said no, I could do more for them independently. He said he didn't have the case files but would get back to me in a few days.

I shook his hand, gave him another card and said, "I'll phone you in about ten days to see how

> *I had the list of questions and answers Vickie had told us to expect in interviews. The attorneys' questions matched that list almost verbatim.*

things are going. In the meantime, if you have any more questions at all, please call me."

As I started to leave, his partner said, "I do have a few more questions. Do you have time?" Not wanting to look desperate, I checked my watch, then agreed I had half an hour.

But I left without a case in hand. My heart fell to the floor. On the way home, I chalked it up to experience, but I kept telling myself, "It'll work, it'll work." Three days later, the firm's paralegal called to say they had four cases waiting for me to pick up.

I Was Instantly So Busy, I Didn't Know Where to Start

I arrived at their offices to find four boxes and a $3,000.00 retainer check. My heart rate was about 250. I actually had cases to work—and a check.

Before I could get out the door with the boxes, one attorney asked to see me about another case. In addition to my other CLNC® services, he needed an expert witness. I told him my fee for finding an expert, then remembered a friend who would be perfect. I gave him that name for free. He offered to pay, but I said, "No, this one's on me. You can pay for the next one."

Once again, I called the Institute. The CLNC® Mentor told me to pace myself, which I did. I finished the cases, and the attorneys were thrilled with my work.

I heard nothing for a couple of days, which felt like months. Then another attorney called with a

> *The law firm called to say they had four cases waiting for me to pick up…. I arrived at their offices to find four boxes and a $3,000.00 retainer check.*

"simple nursing home case" for me to review. I picked it up, spent a couple of hours reviewing it and called to tell him the case had merit. He asked me to put that in a memo.

This time I got out my CLNC® Certification Program materials. Vickie has included everything I need. I used the memo form, typed up the memo and sent it off.

I Received 24 Cases from One Attorney All at Once

I was so busy with cases in November that my husband agreed I should do the legal nurse consulting full time and stop working at the hospital. Come December, all the cases were finished and no calls were coming in. In a major panic, I called the Institute. The CLNC® Mentor told me most attorneys don't do a lot during the holidays. That made sense. I decided not to worry. My husband and I went to California to see his family for Christmas. When we returned, I made my New Year's resolution to continue marketing, no matter what.

The first week of January, I received a call from the attorney who had hired me for those first two cases three years earlier. When I told him my new rates, he said, "That's kind of steep." Again, I sat on my hands. Finally, he said, "All right, I have a list of cases I want you to review."

I expected he would give me five or six cases at most. He gave me 24.

My Next Goal Is a Six-Figure Income

Vickie is so right when she says, "We are nurses and we can do anything®"! We can. We always sell ourselves short, but whatever we set our minds to, we can do. All I did was follow Vickie's advice, use her materials and ask to speak to a CLNC® Mentor whenever I panicked.

My husband and I are going to Hawaii next week. I don't have to check with anyone. As a nurse, I never could have achieved that feeling of independence and freedom.

In six months, I've worked 36 legal nurse consulting cases. I'm on a roll now, and my next CLNC® goal is to make a six-figure income. With everything I've learned from Vickie, I know I can do it.

In six months, I've worked 36 legal nurse consulting cases.... My next CLNC® goal is to make a six-figure income. With everything I've learned from Vickie, I know I can do it.

I Made More Money in 2 Months as a CLNC® Consultant Than in 12 as a Hospital Nurse

by Pamela Erwin, RN, BSN, MS, CLNC, California

> " *I love what I'm doing! In spite of...injuries and pain from a couple of car wrecks, I have achieved professional success and financial independence as a Certified Legal Nurse Consultant*CM. "

I love what I'm doing! In spite of, or actually because of, injuries and pain from a couple of car wrecks, I have achieved professional success and financial independence as a Certified Legal Nurse ConsultantCM.

I've done just about everything in nursing—pediatrics, emergency trauma and cardiac intensive care. I also earned an MS in counseling and became interested in the healing benefits of alternative health-care methods. I changed my lifestyle as well as my family's through diet, meditation, yoga and *tai chi*.

When injuries from a car accident sidelined me for six months, I took a more accommodating position as director of professional services for a girl's reformatory. Another wreck proved to be a real life-changing event. The injuries to my jaw, shoulder, neck and right arm forced me to move to a hot, dry climate.

Meanwhile, someone showed me literature from the Institute's CLNC® Certification Program. I was very impressed and thought, "Boy, they're on target. This is really interesting." Having served as an expert witness on a few occasions, I already knew how much attorneys didn't know about the medical details of cases.

Upon relocation, I had several attractive offers, but I couldn't work a normal 8- to 10-hour day. I realized that legal nurse consulting was my solution. I found the Institute's website and read up on the CLNC® Certification Program. Vickie's program really hit home with me. I became highly motivated to pursue a career as a Certified Legal Nurse Consultant℠.

If I Could Make Millions for Others, I Could Do It for Myself, Too

I knew I had the background to succeed as a CLNC® consultant, but I was scared. My biggest fear was financial. How could I become financially independent, especially in light of my physical limitations? I became determined to get past the pain from my injuries.

I was also fearful about being on my own and not being around my colleagues. Vickie's free CLNC® Mentoring Program was very helpful, and I knew its importance from my counseling background. Even today, I still contact the Institute, especially when I have a challenging case.

Although I'd been consulting for two years, going from a fixed salary to doing it all on my own was a big step for me. But I realized I'd consulted on six start-ups and made millions of dollars for others, so why couldn't I do it for myself? Of course, that's the theme of Vickie's message.

Vickie's free CLNC® Mentoring Program was very helpful... Even today, I still contact the Institute, especially when I have a challenging case.

I ordered the CLNC® Home-Study Certification Program and studied daily for three months, working at it like an eight-hour shift. I went through the course three times. When I took the exam at a local testing center, the Institute helped me get special accommodation to move around because I couldn't sit for that long. Actually, my arm was numb during the exam, and after I got home, I cried in pain— but I passed with flying colors.

I Marshaled One Case to Full-Time CLNC® Success

I was ready to go. I got a couple of consulting jobs from friends of friends—I made $2,000.00 on one case and $5,000.00 on another. My first big assignment came about because of my own door-to-door, out-of-the-phone-book efforts.

Two months after I submitted my marketing packet to one attorney, he called for an interview. After another two months he left a message on my answering machine. Two friends of his law firm's owner had been badly injured in a car wreck. They were in a hospital that had many malpractice lawsuits pending against it, and the owner was afraid his friends, both comatose, would not survive there. The attorney asked me to meet him and his boss at the hospital and review the situation, or as they put it, "marshal the case."

I went in daily and discovered that the care the accident victims were receiving was very poor. I could horrify you for an hour with what I saw and how I intervened. To make a long story short, both victims are okay, although one was in rehab for six weeks, and the case settled for a lot of money.

I never intended to be a full-time Certified Legal Nurse Consultant[CM], but I've been full time ever since this case. I started getting a case about every 10 days, and I've hired a CLNC® subcontractor to help. I'm so busy with my current attorney-clients, I don't have time for other law firms.

I made more money in two months as a CLNC® consultant than I made in 12 as a hospital nurse. I charge $150/hr. My attorney-clients often ask for my informal opinion about a medical situation in a case. These informal consultations are also billable at $150/hr.

I make sure my clients receive plenty of benefits from my CLNC® services. The attorneys know I'm a valuable asset to their efforts and have said so. I actually save them a lot of time and money by helping them establish a direction in a case or determine if a case is worth pursuing.

I give the attorneys a thorough grasp of the medical aspects vital to a case. I show them examples to help them relate to seemingly minor details that are actually life and death issues. Rather than just giving them a general understanding that something is wrong, I try to give them a visceral response to the medical malpractice. That's when they really "get it" and can present a strong case.

> *I made more money in two months as a CLNC® consultant than in 12 as a hospital nurse. I charge $150/hr.*

> *The attorneys know I'm a valuable asset to their efforts and have said so.*

Vickie's Recipe Gave Me Independence and Financial Success

My financial goals were to be able to support myself, live independently, not have to worry about my finances, be a philanthropist of sorts and put my kids through college. I also wanted my work to be honorable and ethical, and to uphold my values. In addition to the money, independence and opportunity to work from home, I love my professional relationships with my attorney-clients and the variety of CLNC® services I get to provide.

I attribute my success to my intentions, to focusing my positive energy. My nursing experience has helped a lot, and I have followed Vickie's advice like a recipe.

Although I've never met Vickie, I feel like she and I are two peas in a pod. Judging by her website, the things she's done and the way she talks, I can tell she's incredibly organized. Yet we also share an interest in *feng shui*, which tells me she's not all traditional. You need some untraditional thinking to succeed in this world.

I am very happy helping attorneys help patients who have been abused by the healthcare system. I know from firsthand experience there's a great need for this kind of work.

I still have some of the pain and physical limitations that led me into this field, but I'm having fun now. I have so much money coming in, I don't know what to do with it. I thank Vickie from the bottom of my heart.

Earning $150/hr as a CLNC® Consultant Is Simple and Real

by Margot G. Lintner, RN, CLNC, California

After 16 years of med-surg and 17 years of psych ER, I still love nursing. I wasn't desperate for a change, but I could tell in my gut something wasn't quite right. I was beginning to look for my next challenge. The face of nursing had been changing and working at the hospital was becoming less desirable. I knew I had to protect myself from burning out.

Vickie's Photo Was Asking "What Are You Waiting For?"

During a midnight break, while reading the northern California nursing journal, I saw an advertisement for Vickie Milazzo Institute's CLNC® Certification Program. The more I looked at Vickie's smiling, determined expression and chic, take-charge style, the more intrigued I became.

A few months later I awoke in the middle of the night. Flipping through my nursing journals again, I saw Vickie's picture staring back at me as if to say, "Well, what are you waiting for?"

I woke my husband and showed him the ad, telling him I was really interested in Vickie's CLNC®

Certification Program. To my surprise, rather than rolling over with a half-hearted, "That's nice, dear," he sat up in bed. Before I knew it, still in our pajamas, we were on the computer visiting LegalNurse.com.

An hour later we were still discussing Vickie's program. By the wee hours I had decided to purchase the VIP CLNC® Success System. "You'll be great at this," my husband declared. "You're going first class, all the way." And so I set my course.

The next day I called Vickie Milazzo Institute and enrolled. Within a few days the CLNC® Home-Study Certification Program arrived. I was more excited than Imelda Marcos in a shoe store.

The day before my 52nd birthday, I left for the CLNC® 6-Day Certification Seminar. What a great gift to give myself, my career, my future and my family. I studied passionately and with pride earned my CLNC® Certification.

Using Vickie's 25 Success Steps Created Instant Success

When I returned home, I immediately practiced the "25 Steps to CLNC® Success" just as Vickie taught. I followed the suggestions in my Advanced CLNC® Practice-Building Program. I created my slogan, got a business phone, put my promotional packet together and went into downtown San Francisco to be fitted for my first-ever business suit. I was ready to go.

The results were immediate. I mailed out seven promotional packets and two attorneys called back. Thrilled and terrified at the same time, I practiced my attorney-client interview with my husband so often he should have earned an honorary law degree.

I hoped and believed I was ready to meet with my first attorney-client. Before leaving for that appointment, I put on my CLNC® pin. I confidently carried my brand new briefcase, affirming I would bring home my first case. I had printed up a contract for services with the date and fees already typed in. I had my sample work products ready.

In that first interview my unique touch was to be 100% me. You see, I come from a long line of Irish lawyers and French restaurateurs, and my grandmother gave me a way to make myself memorable to prospects. I walked in with a pound cake and a "thank you in advance" note.

I left an hour later with the case, retainer and signed contract, plus three referrals. I couldn't believe it. I got in my car, drove a few blocks, took off my shiny new shoes and screamed with delight. In my thoughts I thanked Vickie, the Institute's CLNC® Mentors and my grandmother Marguerite. I couldn't wait to tell my family.

I Expect to Walk Out of the Attorney's Office with a Case

My good fortune has continued growing steadily. I keep sending out my mailings and keep riding my horse forward. Using Vickie's 3-foot rule, I've passed out more cards than a dealer in Vegas.

> *The results were immediate. I mailed out seven promotional packets and two attorneys called back.*

> *I left... with the case, retainer and signed contract, plus three referrals.*

My next stop was the *NACLNC®* Conference, which gave me some great ideas. I came home with a fire inside. As a result, I'm now preparing for three cases from a new attorney-client. My fee is $150/hr and I received a $2,000.00 retainer for each case.

This is turning out to be a great year. In the words of my daughter, I love being a CLNC® consultant "more than a fat boy loves chocolate cake." My success is based on Vickie's basic principles:

▶ First of all, keep it simple. When I meet with an attorney-prospect, I am just "myself."

▶ I make it a point to reflect the attorney. If I can tell he's a little playful, I make a joke or two. If he's all business, so am I. If I see pictures of kids on the desk, they become a brief topic of conversation. I never push it, but I'm very aware of how the attorney presents himself.

▶ I gently let the attorney know I plan to work for her. I always bring a small baked good and a "thank you in advance" note. Even before our interview I decide to believe she will give me cases. I also have my paperwork in order with a prepared contract ready to be signed.

▶ Finally, I stay humble and grateful for my successes. To the entire team at Vickie Milazzo Institute, "Thank you." To the CLNC® Mentors, "Thank you." To Vickie, a special "Thank you."

Yes, Vickie, you were right from day one. I can do this. We can all do this. We can be successful CLNC® consultants if we remember to keep it real, keep it humble and keep it successful.

Here's to your success as a Certified Legal Nurse Consultant℠!

We can be successful CLNC® consultants if we remember to keep it real, keep it humble and keep it successful.

After Only 3 Months Following Vickie's System, I'm a Full-Time CLNC® Consultant

by Tanya Sanderson, RN, BSN, RCIS, CLNC, Tennessee

My CLNC® success happened faster than I imagined it could. The CLNC® 6-Day Certification Seminar and 2-Day NACLNC® Apprenticeship gave me everything I needed. I learned how to write the letters, mail them out, make the follow-up phone calls and get appointments with attorneys. I was totally prepared.

Vickie Taught Me Everything

I sent out eight letters the first time, then nine. I received so many cases, I had to hold off on further marketing until I got them under control. Not that they were really out of control. From the report writing section of the 2-Day NACLNC® Apprenticeship, I knew how to review cases for merit and write my reports. I've done several chronologies. Most of my cases are medical malpractice, but I've also done a workers' comp case.

When I first returned from the CLNC® 6-Day Certification Seminar, I met with a business advisor. Everything he told me to do I had already learned from Vickie. My husband would talk to business people he knew, then ask me, "Did you do this?" I'd say, "Yes, honey. Vickie taught me everything."

I tell my attorney-clients that anytime I have a question I can't answer, I have unlimited access to 6,000 Certified Legal Nurse Consultants^{CM} who have all the collective knowledge I could ever need. It's reassuring to know the CLNC® Mentors are there, too. When I encounter an issue, I'm always impressed with the depth and value of their answers and guidance.

Only one week after the CLNC® 6-Day Certification Seminar I met with my first attorney-prospect and walked out of his office with two cases. I took that as a sign and turned in my resignation at the hospital.

I'm the Attorney's "Expert!"

When my first attorney-client found out I had resigned from my nursing job, he promised to do all he could to help my CLNC® practice grow. He's given me several cases and a referral. Another attorney has done the same.

I called one of these referrals and left a message, but didn't hear back. Then one day, on a whim, I stopped by her office. That turned out to be one of the most exciting events since I started my business.

"I'm so glad you came by," she said and mentioned the attorney who referred me. "When I asked him to help me on this case, he told me his expert would need to review it first."

I received so many cases, I had to hold off on further marketing.

My husband would talk to business people he knew, then ask me, 'Did you do this?' I'd say, 'Yes, honey. Vickie taught me everything.'

> *I got started in December and by the end of February had built a flourishing CLNC® business. All I did was take Vickie's advice— and follow it.*

A moment later it hit me—*I* was the expert. My attorney-client had called me an "expert."

My Husband Looks at Me Differently

Every day I love my new CLNC® business more. I work at home, take my daughter out to lunch and come and go as I please. Weekends are spent with my family. I attend Saturday-night ball games and never miss a Sunday at church. For the past two years at the hospital, I worked on Christmas Eve and Christmas Day, which are big events when you have small children. Now I'll never have to work another holiday.

My husband even looks at me differently. In many ways, I'm a country girl. I love gardening in my jogging pants with a bandana on my head and no makeup. Now I wear business suits, I get my hair done and wear makeup every day. I look and feel professional. Sometimes I catch my husband watching me as if I'm a new person in his life. He's my best friend, and he's always been respectful, but now he shows me a different kind of respect, an intellectual respect. I see that in my attorney-clients too, and it's nice.

Following Vickie's System, Any Certified Legal Nurse Consultant℠ Can Succeed

At the *NACLNC®* Conference, I realized how quickly my success had occurred. After being certified in October, I got started in December and by the end of February had built a flourishing CLNC® business.

All I did was take Vickie's advice—and follow it. Everything I learned in the CLNC® 6-Day Certification Seminar and 2-Day *NACLNC*® Apprenticeship paid off. My money and my time were definitely well spent. Each day, I took one action step toward creating my business, even if it was only going to the office supply store and buying staples. Vickie said, "Just go for it," and I did.

I'll continue to go for it. As a nurse, I specialized in cardiology. Now I'm learning even more about other disease processes that I learned about in nursing school. Being a CLNC® consultant is an amazing new adventure.

Although I've already tucked away enough money to pay the bills for three months, I feel confident that the cases will never stop pouring in. I believe any Certified Legal Nurse Consultant^CM can be equally successful—you just have to follow Vickie's system and take one action step every day toward your CLNC® success just like Vickie teaches.

Everything I learned in the CLNC® 6-Day Certification Seminar and 2-Day NACLNC® Apprenticeship paid off. My money and my time were definitely well spent.

> *A client paid a $40,000 invoice, and we topped that million-dollar goal by $3,000. It was a very exciting day.*

My CLNC® Certification Helped Push My Business Past the $1-Million Mark

by Joy Barry, RN, MEd, CLNC, Massachusetts

When I was a young girl, my family owned a nursing home, so I had a lot of experience with elder care and end-of-life care. I've been in long term care, elder care, end-of-life care and holistic nursing for 25 years, and during that time became director of nursing for a nursing home. When I made the transition into hospice care, I was able to draw on all my previous nursing experience. I went on to earn my master's degree and became CEO of a large, successful hospice program in the Southwest.

Owning my own company was a natural evolution. Today, I'm a full partner in a hospice consulting company that provides both products and services to hospices nationally. When I joined the company in 2000, it was just me and my business partner in a home-based office. We now have a staff of six.

We help hospices with claim denials and fraud investigations by reviewing medical records to evaluate eligibility. Our most exciting assignments have been Medicare antitrust suits, and fraud and abuse suits. We also participated in creating one of the first national corporate integrity agreements for hospice providers.

Vickie Equipped Me with the Skills and Confidence to Exceed My $1-Million Goal

Last year, I became a Certified Legal Nurse Consultant^{CM}. The CLNC® Certification Program gave me the skill and confidence to speak with attorneys, and to market myself and my expertise, as well as my company.

I consider Vickie one of my mentors. She taught me the importance of putting my message out there. Vickie's training also equipped me to discern how I can provide what the attorney needs. Vickie helped me sharpen my skills at determining the merits of a case for either plaintiff or defense. I now know I can provide the best possible CLNC® services to my attorney-clients, regardless of which side of the aisle they're on.

I have also benefited from the CLNC® Mentors. When I came up against questions and wasn't certain about the answers, I contacted the Institute. I have been very impressed with the responsiveness of the staff at Vickie Milazzo Institute and with the CLNC® Mentors.

2006 was our first $1-million year. At the beginning of that year I told my business partner that this was the year we'd break the $1-million mark. She didn't believe me, but all year, I kept saying it. On the last business day of 2006, she came into my office and said, "We didn't do it." The mail had come for the day, we had no more deposits to

Vickie taught me not to live a fear-based life, but to discover what I want to achieve and to go for it.

I have an amazing job and I have many, many blessings in my life as a result of becoming a CLNC® consultant, stepping into my authentic self and not hiding from my dreams.

make, and we were just shy of $1 million. Then at 4:00pm, we got a FedEx delivery. A client paid a $40,000 invoice, and we topped that million-dollar goal by $3,000. It was a very exciting day.

When I Took a Step Toward My Dreams, My Dreams Moved Closer to Me

When I started in nursing school 25 years ago, I realized, like Vickie, that the nursing process we were taught could apply to anything we do. You do a thorough assessment and make a plan, then you intervene by implementing your plan and evaluate by checking back to see if there's anything else you can learn or improve. That's how you achieve any goal. I've taken that part of my nursing training with me in all avenues of my life.

I also believe in Vickie's philosophy of "leap and the net will appear." That's something she taught in the CLNC® 6-Day Certification Seminar and also in her book, *Inside Every Woman: Using the 10 Strengths You Didn't Know You Had to Get the Career and Life You Want Now.* Being fear-based for much of my life, I saw how I held myself back from reaching goals. Vickie taught me not to live a fear-based life, but to discover what I want to achieve and to go for it.

Seven years ago when I first started with my business partner, I couldn't have told you that today I'd be working with six staff members, but here I am. I can't convey how exciting that is. I have an amazing job and I have many, many blessings in my life as a result of becoming a CLNC® consultant, stepping into my authentic self and not hiding from my dreams. When I make those dreams concrete, when I put them on paper, claim them and take that one small step each day, as Vickie taught, I move closer to my dreams, but my dreams also move closer to me. You pledge to take those steps, and before you know it, you're there.

When I make those dreams concrete, when I put them on paper, claim them and take that one small step each day, as Vickie taught, I move closer to my dreams, but my dreams also move closer to me.

I Made $142,000 in My First Year—Part Time

by Lynn Hydo, RN, MBA, CLNC, New York

I've worked in New York hospitals for 20 years, in surgical ICU and critical care. Before I became a Certified Legal Nurse Consultant[CM], I was already reviewing cases to help my boss. He took all the credit and enjoyed all the success. A colleague suggested I enroll in the CLNC® Certification Program and become an independent CLNC® consultant. I did, and since then, tremendous things have happened.

My CLNC® training taught me to focus. Instead of spending time on irrelevant research—looking for a needle in a haystack—I learned to get to the heart of a case quickly. I know how to single out the key elements. Attorneys appreciate this, and I've stayed busy completing a case a week. In my first year as a part-time CLNC® consultant, I did about 50 cases at an average of nearly $3,000.00 per case.

Caring for Attorneys the Way I Care for My Patients Keeps Them Coming Back

I've done a little marketing—business cards, Christmas cards, a few Christmas gifts to my biggest clients—but most of my business comes through referral. Word of mouth is the best. All it takes to generate referrals is giving your attorney-clients the same individualized care you'd give a patient.

If an attorney needs information on a particular product, disease or other subject, I can find it. For one of my cases I did extensive research on a rare germ found in a patient. But hands down, my most popular CLNC® service is the chronology—that's what I deliver most often.

If a case is time sensitive, I push it to the head of the queue. I can turn a case around in less than a week, working on it day and night, if that's what my attorney-client needs. Providing this kind of service wins me repeat business as well as good referrals.

I Used to Come Up Short Financially—Now I'm a Woman of Means

Succeeding as a CLNC® consultant takes perseverance, not only when business is good and you have more work than time, but also when your desk is empty and you wonder if you'll get another case.

Before I became a CLNC® consultant, I was doing all right financially, but occasionally I came up a little short when it was time to pay the mortgage. Now I'm a woman of means. The most exciting thing that's happened to me is watching that balance grow in my business bank account. I can hardly believe it's real—$142,000.00.

I know my business will get even better over time. When you do a good job, there's always another case around the corner. Someday I'll consider becoming a full-time CLNC® consultant, but for now part time is paying off big. I finally have a bank account that makes me feel secure. What's more exciting than that?

I finally have a bank account that makes me feel secure. What's more exciting than that?

I Make the Rules and I've Tripled My Income

by Colleen Galligan, RN, BSN, CDDN, CLNC, Florida

What's amazing about the CLNC® Certification Program is that Vickie teaches you absolutely everything you need to know and gives you all the tools to succeed. The most important thing she told me was to use the CLNC® Mentors.

I can walk into an attorney's office knowing nothing about the case and come out with the assignment. Then I contact Vickie Milazzo Institute, and a CLNC® Mentor is always able to help me sort it out. I ask all my questions, even if I think they're stupid, get the answers and the attorney thinks I'm brilliant.

The other thing Vickie told us was to stick together. If everybody succeeds, then we all do better. This is the only job I've ever had where people in the business really want to help each other. You won't find that anyplace else.

I relocated from New York to Florida. Unemployment can be a great motivator, so I decided to go for it all the way as a Certified Legal Nurse Consultant℠. I figured out what I had to earn to replace my nursing salary, $58,000 a year, with my 20 years of experience in developmental disabilities. To equal that as a CLNC® consultant, I only needed to work six to eight hours a week. I did the math three times to believe it, and I knew it was attainable.

I Creatively Turned "No" into "Yes"

I sent out introductory letters and got creative in responding to "no": "It's been nice meeting you. Maybe I'll see you across the table. Do you know anyone else I should talk to?"

Eventually, "no" started turning into "yes." The first time that happened was one of the most fun days I can remember. As I walked into the courtroom to sit in on a plaintiff case, I recognized the attorney across the table. Not long before, he had told me I overcharged and he would never be interested. When he spotted me, the expression on his face was priceless. The next day he called. It's fun to hear "no" turn to "yes, please"!

I'm proud to say that my first three clients are still my best clients. I landed them by sending out letters, knocking on doors, showing up and being nice to paralegals. I know my clients need and appreciate my CLNC® services.

Once my CLNC® business took off, I got into networking, and my business multiplied even faster. I'm the only CLNC® consultant in my networking group, and each week I meet at least 50 people. Now instead of knocking on an attorney's front door, I go in through the back door—by referral from a golf partner, bridge partner or next-door

I got into networking, and my business multiplied even faster. Once I get in with one attorney, they send me to others.

I work only 25 to 30 hours a week, and I earn three times what I'd be making as a full-time, 60-hour-a-week nurse.

neighbor. Once I get in with one attorney, they send me to others.

After Only a Year I'm Free to Take Off Whenever I Want

A year after moving to Florida, I work only 25 to 30 hours a week, and I earn three times what I'd be making as a full-time, 60-hour-a-week nurse. I provide my own benefits, but the perks are huge. I make the rules. I can do high-quality work in my pajamas. It's my choice, and that's unbelievable freedom.

After spending a lot of years attached to a beeper and cell phone, I love the fact that I don't carry a beeper. Anyone who wants me can leave a message and I'll get back to them.

If I want to work 16 hours a day, I can. If I want to take off in the middle of the day and go see a movie, I can do that, too. When I lived in Manhattan, I never had time to see a Broadway show. Now, if my husband comes home and says, "It's a beautiful day. Let's go to the beach," I can go. I have three cruises and two additional vacations planned for the coming year.

Through Referrals I'm Making Money Faster Than I Ever Expected

I thought I'd be doing medical malpractice cases, but two personal injury attorneys opened their doors to me and gave me my first cases. I figured out what they needed and gave it to them. The

I make the rules. I can do high-quality work in my pajamas. It's my choice, and that's unbelievable freedom.

If I want to take off in the middle of the day and go see a movie, I can.

basis of my business is a report I developed for one of my first personal injury clients. As we discussed his case, I could tell he didn't quite understand what I was saying about my CLNC® services. I told him, "It sounds like you want the good, the bad and the ugly," just as Vickie teaches. He replied, "That's exactly what I want." He called the next week to say, "I love that report. It's great."

I later learned that he shared my report with other attorneys. One morning while I was still in my pajamas, I got a call from an attorney I'd never met. He said, "I need one of those GBUs." I didn't know what he was talking about, so I asked how he got my name. That's when I figured it out—he wanted the good, the bad and the ugly.

Now I have lots of attorneys asking for my "GBU" reports. They're three to five pages long and take five to ten hours to complete. I do five or ten GBUs a week, and they're really fun.

My CLNC® business didn't develop exactly as I had planned. I do personal injury, not medical malpractice. I'm making more money faster than I ever expected, and I love it. I love the work, I love the freedom, I love my clients and I love Vickie Milazzo Institute for showing me how to make it happen.

I have three cruises and two additional vacations planned for the coming year.

I'm making more money faster than I ever expected, and I love it.

I Got Over "I'm Just a Diploma Grad" to Rise Up and Become a Successful Certified Legal Nurse Consultant℠

by Julie R. Gunn, RN, CLNC, Indiana

I graduated from nursing school 33 years ago, when a diploma RN program was anything but the dinosaur it is today. My program included a large amount of clinical experience, which was of great benefit in getting my clinical nursing career started.

After being single until age 38, I met and married my husband. He was 41, previously unmarried and had no children. As a result, we began infertility treatment. After enduring 2½ years of every fertility treatment known to man, our third in vitro fertilization resulted in a pregnancy. I became a mother for the first time at the age of 42. This kept my mind off my growing dissatisfaction with my nursing career.

After 30 Years in Nursing I Was Feeling Stagnant

When I hit the 30-year mark in nursing, I began to feel stagnant. I was just putting in the time. As a diploma RN, I could not teach in a nursing program, nor was I qualified for upper level management in the hospital where I worked. At over 50, returning to school for a nursing degree was out of the question for me.

I felt my 30 years in nursing had been for naught and that I would forever be "just a diploma grad" who could never rise above floor nurse. The following months were filled with feelings of worthlessness, eventually leading to a diagnosis of clinical depression. Medication helped, but my mind centered on the thought that I had more to give to the nursing profession. I felt unappreciated and unrecognized for my years of clinical experience.

Subscriptions to nursing magazines were part of my life, as they are for most RNs. However, with the demands of a husband and young son, I never had enough time to actually read them. I'd noticed advertisements for the Vickie Milazzo Institute's CLNC® Certification Program, but I never considered it a possibility for "just a diploma grad." I assumed the Institute only accepted degreed RNs.

Finally, I confided to my husband my desire to do something more within nursing yet without leaving nursing behind. I mentioned Vickie Milazzo Institute, and he said, "Hey, it's a toll-free number. Call them."

The Opportunity to Go for It as a CLNC® Consultant Gave Me Boundless Joy and Confidence

When I called the Institute, I was shocked that a real person answered the phone, not an answering machine. She was truly interested in me, even though I had no intention of buying anything. My joy was boundless when I heard that a univer-

I really wanted to do this right and felt the VIP CLNC® Success System was the best program for me. I also boosted my learning by attending the NACLNC® Apprenticeship.

In three months since opening my CLNC® business, I have received cases from eight different attorneys.

sity nursing degree was not required to become a Certified Legal Nurse Consultant^CM. She offered to have a full-time practicing CLNC® consultant call me at home. Much to my surprise, this successful CLNC® professional contacted me later that same day. Instead of giving me a sales pitch, she was very up front with me about describing the career of a Certified Legal Nurse Consultant^CM. After that call I took the time to thoroughly research the Institute's program.

I opted for the VIP CLNC® Success System in order to have access to unlimited CLNC® Mentoring. I really wanted to do this right and felt the VIP CLNC® Success System was the best program for me. I also boosted my learning by attending the *NACLNC®* Apprenticeship.

After completing my training and passing the CLNC® Certification Exam, the CLNC® world opened up for me. Each passing day gives me more confidence and the impetus to move forward in my new CLNC® career. In three months since opening my CLNC® business, I have received cases from eight different attorneys and more than one case from three of them. Financially speaking, I have been blessed to make $15,000 in three months. By the end of this year, I will, most likely, equal or surpass my previous salary working at the hospital. I never expected to do this well so soon.

I approach every case with anticipation, not feelings of inadequacy and dread. I look forward to what each case will teach me. I also look forward to educating the attorney when indicated and assisting her toward the very best possible outcome for her client.

Attorneys need and appreciate my nursing knowledge and assessment skills. As a result, I no longer feel like "just a diploma grad." I know that Vickie is right—"I am a nurse and I can do anything!"

> *I never expected to do this well so soon.*

Get on the Fast Track to Success with Vickie's Programs

by Jean A. Hoepfel, RN, PhD, CLNC, Texas

I may hold the record for attending the most Vickie Milazzo programs. I went to my first seminar in 1993 after receiving a brochure in the mail. I wanted to get into legal nurse consulting, but I accepted a job in East Texas and was too busy. I attended my next conference in 1994, but was in the middle of my doctoral dissertation, so I again put CLNC® work on hold. I went to the *NACLNC®* Conference in 1995, but I still wasn't ready. Finally, after the 1997 *NACLNC®* Conference, I made the jump into the world of legal nurse consulting.

Start with a Bang

I started full time by devoting 40+ hours a week to developing CLNC® my business. I had only six months of "staying power" (savings to live on). I wanted everything in place before I opened my doors to all those lawyers. I didn't do any marketing since I was too busy putting my business plan together and gathering my work materials.

My first case came from a neighbor, a lawyer inexperienced in personal injury cases. Once I had confidence that I could do the work and could say I was an "experienced" CLNC® consultant, I started attending legal conferences where I could schmooze with attorneys to market my services and myself.

This worked quite well and is my main marketing strategy today.

Develop a Satisfying Specialty

After a few PI and medical malpractice cases, I decided to pursue Fen-Phen litigation cases since I had 20+ years' experience in cardiovascular and preventive medicine, as well as a doctorate in epidemiology. I read everything I could find about diet drugs and their alleged health consequences and developed a large database of scientific articles. I called my lawyer and judge friends and asked for recommendations, attended more legal conferences and finally got a call from a law firm in Houston. They were looking for an epidemiologist to help with causation and scientific evidence issues. For the past 1½ years I have consulted with this law firm and others about diet drug litigation and other products liability issues.

My company specializes in assessing causation between exposure to potentially harmful substances and poor health outcomes. We analyze the scientific literature for methodological problems or inaccurate conclusions. We also locate and prepare testifying experts on these issues.

Get Lean

Initially I had a home office. I started with the dining room, engulfed the guest bedroom and finally took over the master bedroom. That worked okay since I was the only full-time employee, although I had two part-time employees. I liked working in my running clothes without makeup. I

"I could not have entered this field without Vickie Milazzo Institute's Certification Program."

> *I wanted to get on the fast track and was willing to do whatever it took to leapfrog over those who are still wondering how to start.*

loved sending out emails when I got up at 4:00am, just to show the attorneys what a hard worker I was (but I never sent any out after 9:00pm when I was sound asleep!).

When I started adding full-time staff, I realized I needed an outside office (actually, they coerced me). Recently we moved to a real office suite with three private offices, a storeroom and our "war room," and I could not be happier. I like being able to leave my work behind (rather than in the room at the end of the hall). I still often work seven days a week and 10-12 hour days, especially before trial, but I love it. I really love having my home back without my employees and their work spread out all over the place.

Tap into the Entrepreneurial Spirit

In my "former life" I had my own independent nursing practice for 14 years providing exercise therapy, disease management and personal training. However, I wanted to use my epidemiology background as well as my nursing skills in a more challenging way. On three different occasions I tried to work for a hospital or research company, but I could not tolerate working for someone else and going to mandatory meetings that only wasted my time.

I have always viewed myself as an entrepreneur, relished competition and challenges, and most important, preferred working on my own. I have always been driven and motivated. After all I am a first-born child, and my parents are German (complete with strong work ethic).

I truly enjoy learning and continue to take post-doctoral studies in epidemiology and public health, as well as holding a faculty position at a school of public health. I read motivational books and magazines. I try to surround myself with successful, driven people and stay away from "toxic" people who drain me.

Take the Fast Track to CLNC® Success

In spite of my background, I could not have considered entering this field without attending Vickie Milazzo Institute's CLNC® Certification Program and purchasing *all* the Institute's educational materials. I wanted to get on the fast track and was willing to do whatever it took to leapfrog over those who are still wondering how to start.

I believe that you must make a financial and emotional commitment if you want to succeed in this business. In less than a year, I reached my financial goal, achieving that magic six-figure income. I immediately plowed most of that back into my company to grow even more successful.

My suggestions for those of you entering this field are:

1. Attend more than one of Vickie Milazzo Institute's programs and purchase all their educational materials. This is a small investment for starting a potentially very profitable business on the fast track.

You must make a financial and emotional commitment if you want to succeed in this business.

In less than a year, I reached my financial goal, achieving that magic six-figure income.

Vickie Milazzo Institute's programs... [are] a small investment for starting a potentially very profitable business on the fast track.

2. Attend legal conferences. Use local conferences for schmoozing and others for education and more schmoozing.

3. Ask friends, family and colleagues for referrals and introductions to potential clients.

4. Learn as much as you can about starting a business.

5. Let your education and experience work for you.

6. Take care of yourself and, most important, believe in yourself.

7. Remember—inch by inch, anything's a cinch.

Good luck and work hard—it's worth it.

Use Vickie's Proven Strategies for Your Own CLNC® Success

I Love Defining My CLNC® Success on My Own Terms

by Leana Peterson-Leaf, RN, CLNC, Illinois

I n high school I dreamed of traveling the world and unraveling mysteries untold. I wanted to be an investigative reporter. My only problem was that I was too shy to talk to strangers. So I went into nursing school to make a difference. Ironically, I found the courage not only to talk to strangers, but to ask them the most embarrassing questions about their bodily functions.

Over the course of my nursing career, I went from proud new nurse paying my dues on the night

I knew Vickie Milazzo Institute's program is based on sound, ethical business practices and is delivered with integrity.

123

I had fulfilled my dream of being a nurse and an investigative reporter. I have the best of both worlds.

shift, to the top of the pay scale in hemodialysis. After spending more than 15 years in this specialty, and weathering the storms of managed care and downsizing, I found myself underpaid, overworked and undervalued. I was traveling the path I had most resisted, becoming a burned out nurse.

My CLNC® Certification Launched My Invigorating Trip to Success

For a number of years, I'd been planning to become a legal nurse consultant, but my plans were cast in Jello. Then I learned about Vickie Milazzo Institute's CLNC® Certification Program, and I had, as Oprah would say, my "Aha!" moment. I knew that Vickie Milazzo Institute's program was based on sound, ethical business practices and it is delivered with integrity. I had fortitude, persistence and faith in myself and in Vickie's principles. How could I fail if I applied those principles?

Becoming a Certified Legal Nurse Consultant^{CM} was my first step toward success. The trip has been invigorating.

When I started my consulting business, I defined success in measurable amounts of money. I quickly learned the *most* gratifying rewards are not tangible. Success comes when you least expect it, and it is not always what you expect.

Success #1: I Have the Best of Both Worlds

My first case was a large medical malpractice suit in a specialty I considered my greatest weakness, cardiac. I took the case anyway. Three hospitals were involved, and all the records were mixed together. It took me six hours just to put them in order. You can imagine how pleased my attorney-client was when I gave him a full report in just 32 pages, including a great deal of research.

This was my first success: Realizing I had fulfilled my dream of being a nurse *and* an investigative reporter. I have the best of both worlds.

Success #2: Self-Respect Is the Best Success of All

The attorney loved my report. His only question was, "What does CCU stand for?" I couldn't believe it. Here was an attorney getting ready to litigate a million-dollar suit, and he didn't even know what CCU means. I told myself, if he has the guts, I have the guts. That was my second success: Respecting and valuing my own abilities.

Success #3: Going for It Makes Everything Else Possible

At first, I practiced part time as a CLNC® consultant, working approximately 20 hours a week while maintaining my full-time home health position and raising four teenagers. I quickly learned I could not devote the attention my CLNC® practice required. Following up with contacts and implementing the many ideas rolling around in my head became difficult.

My husband, a businessman and most supportive partner, said, "Quit your job when you feel the time is right. I'm behind this all the way." That was

I am making money, I feel successful and I love it…. I feel stimulated and enthusiastic about my future.

all I needed to hear. Despite fearing loss of income, change of lifestyle and mostly failure, I stuck my neck out. My third success was finding the courage to go for it.

Success #4: My Value Lies in How I Think and What I Know

I have now been in business for only three years, but the personal and professional achievement I have experienced far exceeds anything I could have imagined. I am intellectually challenged by each new case, stepping out of my box to research and explore unknown territory.

When one regular client gives me a case, he often says, "It's yours. You tell me what to do." This kind of respect is a far cry from being valued for how much I can physically do in an eight-hour shift and how much of my personal time I am willing to give beyond the call of duty. This is my fourth success: I am valued and respected for how I think and what I know.

The Ultimate Success: I'm *Feeling* Successful Doing What I Love

Today, I am making money, I feel successful and I love it. I'm reaching out to attain goals and learning every day. Once again, I feel stimulated and enthusiastic about my future.

As I write this CLNC® Success Story, I'm sitting here in my bathrobe and slippers with my hair a mess. My kids are off to school and my dog is lying on the floor next to me. Around 9:00am the phone will start ringing, and I will be talking to clients who call me because they value my knowledge and expertise.

I am enjoying every step of this journey, both the challenges and the successes, because I am in control of my future. There are no failures in this business. If I don't get the new client, so what? I move on. There are lots of attorneys out there. Failures are merely learning experiences that lead to the next success, and the next.

The moral of my story is this: Doing what you love *is* success. Success is not defined by fortune alone. It doesn't come while you're looking for it. It comes unexpectedly while you're filling the needs of your clients. It arrives in the moment you discover the key to your case and put the last piece of the puzzle in place.

My advice to aspiring Certified Legal Nurse Consultants^CM: Stick your neck out and get busy failing— I mean, learning—so you too can succeed—on your own terms. Enjoy your journey to CLNC® success, because this journey truly has no end.

> *Stick your neck out and get busy... learning— so you too can succeed.*

In Just 8 Months I've Increased My Income 70% as a Certified Legal Nurse Consultant℠

by Lori Lynn, RN, CLNC, Michigan

I first saw an ad for the CLNC® Certification Program in a nursing magazine about five years ago. What sparked my interest was the $125-plus per hour consulting fee I could earn. I have enjoyed nursing for 20 years, but I knew I didn't want to grow old being a hospital nurse. I was feeling a little dissatisfied with the politics, the bureaucracy, the increased patient loads and the administrative problems. Yet if I went to work in a doctor's office or outside the hospital, I felt I would never achieve some of my goals such as traveling. I wanted to increase my income and further my career but stay in a field related to nursing.

I called Vickie Milazzo Institute and requested my free information packet. When the information packet arrived, I read the free *CLNC® Success Stories* book and found it fascinating and exciting. These were nurses like me who became Certified Legal Nurse Consultants℠. Even in the midst of trials and tribulations in their personal lives, they had triumphed and were now successful CLNC® consultants.

For a couple of years I entertained the idea of becoming a CLNC® consultant, but I was going through a divorce, I had an ill parent and this was a trying time in my life. I knew I needed emotional energy to focus on the CLNC® business.

Finally, three years later, my boyfriend, who's a very successful businessman, encouraged me to get certified. Last May I attended the CLNC® 6-Day Certification Seminar and the 2-Day *NACLNC®* Apprenticeship that immediately followed.

I firmly believe that if I had not done the Apprenticeship, I wouldn't be where I am today. It prepared me to go out and market myself. As a nurse, I was so accustomed to serving and helping people that I wasn't used to selling myself. The Apprenticeship program gave me the extra boost of confidence and all the tools I needed to leap into the marketing aspect of my CLNC® business.

In Just 8 Months I Met All My Goals and Increased My Income 70%

When I got home, I started formulating a business plan with one-month, two-month and three-month goals. Like Vickie taught me, I began taking baby action steps every day. One of those baby steps was telling at least three people what I did. When my profession came up in the course of conversation, a lot of people didn't know what Certified Legal Nurse Consultants^CM do. I would explain, and they'd say, "I know an attorney" or "I have a neighbor who's an attorney." This easy networking is directly related to my success today.

I also set a goal to be successful in my CLNC® business by my next birthday, and on my birthday

Within only eight months, I have increased my income by 70%.

I got my first case. Now, I'm retired from the hospital because I couldn't juggle my hospital work with all my CLNC® assignments. That was another goal I met.

I feel like an investigative reporter. I get to look at medical records, piece together what happened and figure out the puzzle. That's fascinating. And within only eight months, I have increased my income by 70%. It's been an exciting journey.

Vickie Is an Incredible Role Model for Me and My CLNC® Business

Vickie is an awesome woman and she's really worked hard to get where she is. Yet she's actually one of us. Her teaching style is fresh, down to earth and easy to follow. She's highly motivating and encouraging. During the CLNC® 6-Day Certification Seminar I found myself just waiting for every word that came out of her mouth. From the time I got certified last May until the *NACLNC®* Conference in March, I was counting the days. I know I wouldn't be here today without her VIP CLNC® Success System.

Legal nurse consulting is a specialized field. After the CLNC® 6-Day Certification Seminar and the 2-Day *NACLNC®* Apprenticeship, I felt fully prepared to put on that power suit and shake hands with that attorney.

Along the way other nurses have been curious about what I've accomplished, and I tell them that Vickie Milazzo Institute offers the only program that helps you flourish as a legal nurse consultant. I know one nurse who did a program online, more of a nurse-paralegal program presenting itself as a legal nurse consulting program. She has never done anything with it because she doesn't have the tools to get started.

Every VIP Resource Gives Me New, Easy-to-Use Ideas

I've made good use of the unlimited mentoring with the CLNC® Mentors. They all know me, and the wonderful thing is, no question seems stupid to them. They're so willing to help you succeed. They understand because they've been there, and they give you great ideas on how to get through whatever obstacle or question you're facing.

The other resources of the VIP CLNC® Success System have also been very helpful—they're like my third, fourth and fifth vitals. I frequently refer to Vickie's books; the *Core Curriculum for Legal Nurse Consulting®* textbook, *Flash 55: 55 FREE Ways to Promote Your CLNC® Business* and *Create Your Own Magic for CLNC® Success,* for fresh ideas on how to enhance my business. All of Vickie's books are well written and easy to follow.

I Have a Fresh Attitude Toward Nursing and a Rewarding New Way to Help Patients

The most rewarding thing about my CLNC® practice is that I get to continue helping patients and their families. In the course of my business, I have met with the attorneys' clients, either a surviving patient or the family of a patient who has passed away. I've actually sat with them, held their hands, listened to their traumatic stories and made

During the CLNC® 6-Day Certification Seminar I found myself just waiting for every word that came out of her mouth.

I've made good use of the unlimited mentoring with the CLNC® Mentors. They understand because they've been there, and they give you great ideas.

friends in the process. Then when the case goes to trial, I've seen their reaction when they recover the damages they deserve for the error that occurred—their satisfaction at receiving justice and their relief that the ordeal is finally over. You can't take away the loss they suffered, but knowing that you were able to help them find satisfaction and make the loss more bearable is very rewarding.

Becoming a Certified Legal Nurse Consultant[CM] has changed my life because it's given me a new, fresh attitude toward nursing, the work nurses do, and the incredible reward they experience from making someone better as well as the dissatisfaction they feel when they could have done more if they'd had the time. I've actually learned more nursing than I ever would have learned in the hospital because I'm now dealing with adult disease processes and surgery cases in addition to neonatal and pediatric cases which are my specialty. As a CLNC® consultant I have a renewed sense of where I'm going, what I'm doing and what I'm meant to do, and this profession is a perfect fit for me.

I Achieved Immediate Success Exhibiting at Legal Conferences

by Laura H. Beard, RN, BSN, CLNC, South Carolina

Vickie, I just have to tell you about my recent exhibiting success. I started my Certified Legal Nurse Consultant^{CM} business 5½ months ago after a long hiatus from nursing. I was fortunate to be able to work on my legal nurse consulting business full time and I made a concerted effort to use the marketing strategies I learned from the CLNC® Certification Program. I got my first two cases on the same day within a week of my launch date just networking with friends. This networking brought me two attorneys and seven cases in the first three months.

To create immediate success for my legal nurse consulting business, I decided to exhibit at a statewide plaintiff attorney convention. I put to use the event marketing information in the *Core Curriculum for Legal Nurse Consulting*® textbook, *NACLNC*® Apprenticeship and Advanced CLNC® Practice-Building Programs. I decided to spend the money to hire a graphic designer to create a professional tri-fold exhibit I could use repeatedly. I was thrilled with the final product and thanks to the information I received from Vickie Milazzo Institute, my exhibit booth looked attractive and professional.

I got my first two cases on the same day within a week of my launch date just networking with friends.

I stood in front of my exhibit throughout the convention and introduced myself to most everyone who walked by. I passed out numerous business cards and brochures. I focused my conversations on how the attorneys were currently screening and developing their medical-related cases and how I could save them time and money. On the first day, I stayed until all attorneys and all but two exhibitors had left the exhibit hall. Ten minutes after returning to my hotel room, I got a call from an attorney-prospect who was waiting by my booth with medical records for me to review! Needless to say, I ran downstairs to meet with him. Believe it or not, I walked away from that convention with not one but *two* sets of medical records and retainers for both cases from that one attorney!

I received permission to follow up from every attorney with whom I spoke. I also gave free screenings to three attorneys who were particularly interested in my CLNC® services. Two other attorneys asked me to call them after the convention to discuss a case on which they needed help. The day after I notified one attorney of his free screening, he called me to discuss a case he wanted me to handle. He needed help with several cases and wanted to get started. His firm handles a large number of malpractice and negligence cases so this opportunity really opened doors for my CLNC® business.

I was surprised on the second day of the convention when one of the other two legal nurse consultant exhibitors shut down their booth (three RNs were exhibiting together). It was "tax-free shopping" that weekend so they closed their booth at 11:00am and went shopping! Needless to say, they had not achieved the Vickie Milazzo Institute's CLNC® Certification. Since the convention was only 2½ days, they lost a huge opportunity to meet attorneys.

All in all, as a result of exhibiting at this one event I came home with the following:

- Two sets of medical records and retainer fees for each case from the same attorney.
- Requests from two attorneys to call regarding cases on which they need help.
- Request to screen a case for merit from a new attorney-client.
- Request to locate two testifying experts.
- Plus I received the attorney mailing list data base from the association sponsoring the convention.

While exhibiting is not cheap nor easy, it definitely paid off for me. It gave my CLNC® business statewide exposure and I will be hiring my first CLNC® subcontractor to help with my rapidly increasing case load. I love my new career as a Certified Legal Nurse Consultant℠ and look forward to many years of exhibiting success.

I walked away from that convention with not one but two sets of medical records and retainers for both cases.

I love my new career as a Certified Legal Nurse Consultant℠ and look forward to many years of exhibiting success.

CLNC® Certification Paved My Way to Success as an In-House Certified Legal Nurse Consultant℠

by Michelle Tucker,
RN, MSN, CLNC, Florida

I'm certain I couldn't have made it without Vickie's informative, straightforward program.

For 15 years, I was a pediatric critical care clinical specialist for a large Florida county hospital. I also worked as a pediatric critical care expert witness and wanted the additional training Vickie's CLNC® Certification Program offered. After I served as an expert witness on one case, the attorney recruited me for an in-house position with his large medical malpractice defense firm.

The day I left the hospital was the day I ordered the CLNC® Home-Study Certification Program. My goal was to get through the program before I started my new position. I finished the course, took my test, and passed the CLNC® Certification Exam in record time (four weeks exactly).

More important than passing the CLNC® Certification Exam was the knowledge I gained from the program. I took on my new job with confidence. I have been at the law firm for over a year now, and I'm certain I couldn't have made it without Vickie's informative, straightforward program.

My job at the law firm entails many duties, including:

▶ Organizing and summarizing all medical records that come into the office.

▶ Identifying relevant medical issues and new angles in the cases.

▶ Determining the types of expert witnesses needed.

▶ Locating and speaking with expert witnesses.

▶ Writing medical chronologies and timelines.

▶ Writing deposition summaries.

▶ Researching medical literature.

▶ Identifying healthcare providers and witnesses in the discovery process.

I keep my CLNC® Certification Program at my office. When I'm stumped by a question, my CLNC® Success System always gives me the answers.

My boss treats me like gold, and I've never been happier in my career. Vickie's CLNC® Certification Program is worth every penny. It gave me the tools to make it as a Certified Legal Nurse Consultant^CM. I recommend Vickie's program to any nurse who is interested in the field of legal nurse consulting.

When I'm stumped by a question, my CLNC® Success System always gives me the answers.

Vickie's CLNC® Certification Program is worth every penny.

I Am Now Financially Independent
by Barbara Rose, RN, CLNC, Texas

After finishing Vickie's CLNC® 6-Day Certification Seminar, I followed Vickie's marketing instructions to the letter and got my first case in four months. In a little over a year I am financially independent and no longer depend on the hospital.

Since I knew I would specialize in long term care, I sought out attorneys who dealt with long term care and Medicare issues. I sent out marketing packets and received a response that became my first case. That attorney gave my name to two other attorneys, and from those referrals, I received another case.

Networking with a coworker led me to my first regular attorney-client. He in turn recommended me to three more attorneys, and two of them have since become regular clients. I now work with attorneys all over Texas.

When asked to do my first deposition, I went right back to the *Core Curriculum for Legal Nurse Consulting®* textbook, and I felt completely prepared. The attorney and I overwhelmed the opposition, and they settled. The opposing counsel told me, "I never want to be on the opposing side when you're being deposed." That literally put me over the top. I am now comfortable with attorneys because I speak their language. I could only have developed that confidence from the CLNC® Certification Program.

Becoming a Certified Legal Nurse Consultant^{CM} has been a life-changing experience. I never realized this opportunity was out there. Vickie's program gave me the tools I needed to become a CLNC® consultant, from putting reports together, to being deposed, to learning about interrogatories.

Best of all—I get to work from my home. I now have more money, more respect and more free time than I have ever had in my entire life.

I now have more money, more respect and more free time than I have ever had in my entire life.

I'm Living the Good Life as a CLNC® Consultant and Mother

by Jennifer M. Fougerousse, RN, CLNC, Texas

Becoming a Certified Legal Nurse Consul-tant^CM changed my life. I can take my baby to play group, run errands, exercise, cook dinner—and work—all before my husband comes home. I can take a day off whenever I want and go on vacation without asking for time off. I'm living the good life!

Before becoming a CLNC® consultant, I had 18 months of experience in pediatrics and three years working part time in an outpatient surgery recovery room. When I heard about Vickie's fabulous pro-gram, I realized I could use all my nursing skills and experience, yet work at home and more than double my hourly wage. I enrolled in the CLNC® Home-Study Certification Program. Several nights a week, as soon as my daughter went to bed, I'd watch the program. The course is broken down into conve-nient modules, so I could easily plan my schedule.

Start with a Strong Understanding of What the Attorney Needs

Through the CLNC® Certification Program, Vickie gave me a strong basic understanding of the law and showed me how to use that knowledge along with my nursing expertise in analyzing med-ical-related cases. Vickie teaches you to think like a lawyer—what they're looking for, what they need.

When I started my business, an attorney friend became my first client. Two-and-a-half years later he still keeps me busy. I worked for his law firm exclusively until I felt comfortable.

Then I started getting referrals and I went after them, using Vickie's strategies. I am persistent, following up until I actually speak to the attorney-prospect. Attorneys appreciate my patience and persistence. They often say, "I get so busy. I'm so glad you kept calling."

Build Confidence with CLNC® Certification and Support

Part of my confidence comes from the CLNC® Certification. The word "certified" carries a lot of weight with attorneys.

My confidence also comes from having an enthusiastic support group that wants nothing more than for me to succeed. Whenever I call the Institute, everyone is truly eager to hear about my successes. And I get free CLNC® Mentoring. That coaching and support give me the confidence and skills to go out and get more business.

Market Your Way to the Good Life

Recently, I started an information newsletter—another of Vickie's marketing strategies. Three weeks after I sent it out. I got my first call. I've been so busy with my attorney-clients that this is an easy way to market without hitting the streets. I can put my newsletter into attorneys' hands every

> *Part of my confidence comes from the CLNC® Certification. The word 'certified' carries a lot of weight with attorneys.*

three months to remind them I'm here. Later, when they need a legal nurse consultant, they remember that newsletter and call me.

Today I have two daughters, ages 3½ and 10 months. My CLNC® practice has become increasingly busy so I hired a nanny. In the past seven months, I've canceled her only one day. I have never had a slow month.

I earn the same amount of money as I would have working full time at the hospital, but I only have to put in half the hours. I get to work as much or as little as I want. And I have my beautiful girls coloring at my feet while I type a report.

My proudest accomplishments as a CLNC® consultant are starting my business, watching it grow and meeting my first-year goals with ease. I love it when people ask what I do for a living, and I can say, "I own my own business." I couldn't ask for a better life.

Consulting Can Be Criminal

by Laurel Grisbach, RN, California

Many nurses understand how a Certified Legal Nurse Consultant^{CM} can evaluate medical malpractice, workers' compensation and personal injury cases. But few appreciate the possibility of applying CLNC® consulting services to other types of cases.

Recently, I had the opportunity to use my consulting skills in a new area—criminal law. The case that started my new career was the federal civil rights trial of Rodney Glenn King. This high-profile case didn't fall into my lap by accident. If a relatively "green" CLNC® consultant like me can do it, you can too. Here's how I put myself in the right place at the right time.

Rule #1: Prepare Yourself for Success

My journey to "fame" started with the arrival of the postman on my day off. As I halfheartedly went about my routine household chores, I found myself anticipating his arrival, always a pleasant morning break. I was not disappointed. Among the catalogs, bills and junk mail, I found a bright flyer from one of my favorite seminar speakers, Vickie Milazzo. Before I could think twice, the check had filled itself out. Not bad—only a few minutes after the mail came, I had registered for Vickie's program.

Suddenly, I was overcome with uncertainty. How could I justify yet another seminar to my

> *If a relatively 'green' CLNC® consultant like me can do it, you can too.*

husband? You see, I am a seminar-holic. For years I'd been absorbing ways of using my nursing skills other than in direct patient care. I'd return home from these sessions bursting with enthusiasm. Next thing I knew, I'd be so involved in the vicious circle of daily existence I had neither the time nor the energy to plan my career change. My spouse, understanding and supportive as he is, had grown tired of hearing my "Think of This Seminar as an Investment in Our Future" approach and was more than ready for me to put all this education to use.

I finally convinced my husband to back me for "just one last seminar." This time I promised to make a concerted effort to launch my legal nurse consulting practice.

Rule #2: Just Do It!

Once the seminar was over, the hard part began. Three words came to mind: "Just do it!" I've been told that I exude confidence and authority, and I've never doubted that I could be a good consultant. Behind that brave façade, however, I wanted to evaporate, especially when confronted with two undeniable facts:

1. I was the only person in Vickie's seminar who didn't even know an attorney.

2. I had absolutely nothing of interest to put on a curriculum vitae—in fact, before the seminar, I'd never even heard of one. For once, I wished I'd graduated from a

bachelor's program, had more certifications after my name and emergency room experience in the double digits.

My postal service buddy was starting to bother me with his relentless delivery of bills and catalogs. Oh well, I thought, just do it!

While trying to pick a lawyer to be the lucky recipient of my first introductory packet, I recalled the name of the prominent attorney defending one of the officers in the Rodney King/LAPD federal trial. I realized I had only a "snowball's chance" of getting a response from him, but then again, what if I did? I "just did it" and sent him my letter of introduction. Two weeks later I had not heard a word. (In retrospect, I should have followed up on my mailing.)

I had promised my husband an all-out effort, and that was what he was going to get. I requested the roster of the Trial Lawyers Association and began sending out packets. I told myself this was good therapy, as it gave me a new reason to look forward to my postal carrier's visits.

Rule #3: Get Ready to Get Lucky (If You've Followed Rules 1 and 2)

After a month, I'd almost given up on the Rodney King attorney. Then after a horrific day in the ER, I picked up the kids at the sitter and made my 1½-hour drive home. In my mailbox I found a thick manila envelope.

I 'just did it' and sent him my letter of introduction.

I could feel my face flushing the moment I realized I was holding the medical records of Rodney King.

I could feel my face flushing the moment I realized I was holding the medical records of Rodney King. This was unbelievable. I had just landed what was possibly the most controversial case of the decade. I couldn't wait to call everyone I knew and share my good news.

Now what? What if I didn't have anything new to offer the attorneys that they had not already learned during their extensive preparation for the state trial?

Rule #4: Make a Plan and Follow It

With reality staring me in the face, I settled down and formed my game plan. First step—review King's medical records and make a detailed report for my new client. My approach to interpreting the records was wide open. The attorney's only request was that I help in any way I could.

As it turned out, my initial fears were unfounded. A quick glance at the records revealed many holes in the charting and virtually no nurses' notes. Yet none of the physician experts on the state's side had touched on my observations.

From the outset, two main points struck me about King's records: the relatively minor physical injuries he actually sustained; and the massive deviations from standards of care during the initial emergency treatment. My report included the following findings:

▶ The pre-hospital care forms contained several strange entries and omissions. To clarify these inconsistencies, I prepared deposition questions for the paramedics involved.

► The emergency department nurses' notes revealed multiple late entries with virtually no documentation at the time of treatment. I itemized and explained all the deviations from standards of care.

► I explained the existence of the Los Angeles Medic-Alert Center (MAC) and its role in transferring patients from private facilities to county hospitals. Within minutes of learning that all conversations with the MAC are recorded, the attorney applied for a federal subpoena for the recording.

► I compiled a vital signs chart to demonstrate King's relatively unremarkable hospital stay and counseled the attorneys about potential changes in vital signs during times of pain, stress or infection. Then I verbally correlated such changes with documented events.

Rule #5: Use Every Resource to the Max

I considered myself somewhat of a sideline expert on this case as I had watched most of the first trial on *Court TV*. I was aware of the types of information provided by the mega-buck physician experts. The only area already covered in-depth was how King's fractures could have occurred from a fall or a beating. My familiarity with the previous TV coverage confirmed that the case was wide open for my observations.

Vickie was correct: Pieces of information that seemed simple and basic to me were important news to an attorney who had never taken Nursing 101.

My questions brought out many points that made a definite impact on the opposition.

After finishing my report, I scheduled a meeting at the law firm to go over my findings. For two hours the attorney listened intently as I pointed out the most basic nursing practices and observations of which he was totally unaware. (What is a late note? Do emergency records generally have late entries? What does it mean when a nurse draws a line to the end of a page and writes her initials?) My training with Vickie was absolutely correct: Pieces of information that seemed simple and basic to me were important news to an attorney who had never taken Nursing 101.

The Bottom Line: Launch a New Career

Throughout the medical testimony in the federal trial, I was present in the courtroom as a consulting expert. I helped the attorney compile questions to ask during cross-examination. My questions brought out many points that made a definite impact on the opposition. The thrill of throwing the prosecution off balance made staying focused difficult—it's tough not to become engulfed in courtroom strategy when your opposition is frantically shuffling through records to locate some "overlooked detail" you've just helped bring to their attention.

The King case has been called the most publicized trial in 50 years, and I found the immensity of it overwhelming at times. The awe of sitting "in the well" with four of the nation's finest prosecuting attorneys, four highly regarded defense attorneys and four famous defendants will stay with me for years.

Do I feel the police were guilty? It doesn't matter what I think—that was for the jury to decide. My role was simply to explain the medical records in layman's terms and convey what those records meant to the attorney's case.

I do know my attorney-client is now sold on using my services and has been quick to share his discovery with his colleagues.

The bottom line is this: I upheld my end of my bargain with my husband, so you will probably see me around another nursing seminar in the L.A. area. (Now I can afford to pay for it with my own money.) Just look for a tall blonde wearing a big grin and telling everyone, "Just do it!"

My attorney-client is now sold on using my services and has been quick to share his discovery with his colleagues.

Vickie's "Action Steps" Formula Worked for Me

by Guyolyn Smith-Ousterhout,
RNC, CPUR, CLNC, Mississippi

I don't know where to begin other than simply to say, *"Thanks."* I thought I would never retain all the information I received at the CLNC® 6-Day Certification Seminar, let alone put it all into action. When I returned home my quest was to have one client within a month. Initially, I was testing the formula I had learned. If I took daily "action steps" and set up my business exactly as Vickie taught, could it possibly work? I was in for a rewarding surprise.

I began my journey almost immediately after I stepped off the plane. From day one, I worked on my CLNC® consulting practice at least three to four hours a day. Within the next two weeks I had met with my accountant, produced my promotional package, hired someone to build my website and begun, hesitantly, promoting myself (the scariest part).

Less than a month since I started, I am having to request time off from my current position to meet the demands of my attorney-clients. My first assignment was from an attorney who was turning down some cases because of his lack of time to pursue the medical aspects of each case. This attorney's wife, who works with another medical malpractice firm, also requested my card. The same day, I received a call from a workers' compensation attorney who needed help. The next day I received an email from an attorney in the adjoining state who was desperate for a nurse to screen a case for merit. This attorney was referred to me by the first attorney.

This endeavor takes me on a course that is filled with fear and excitement. I am so thankful to Vickie Milazzo Institute for providing me with the knowledge and, most important, the encouragement to go for it and become a successful Certified Legal Nurse Consultant^CM.

Less than a month since I started, I am having to request time off from my current position to meet the demands of my attorney-clients.

I Gained by Investing in My Future

by Donna du Bois,
RNC, MPH, CLNC, Texas

Several of my co-workers took the CLNC® Certification Program and raved about it. All are now Certified Legal Nurse Consultant CM making good money consulting. Two were near retirement and needed additional income to continue their comfortable lifestyles. They are both retired and now earn more than they ever did in their regular jobs.

The program seemed expensive to me, and I decided I didn't need it. Then out of the blue an attorney's office called to ask if I would review some cases. His staff had seen my name on a website and realized from my credentials that I had the long term care expertise they needed. I didn't have a clue what to charge, but the legal nurse consultant hiring me was kind enough to tell me what other consultants charged. I realized I loved working on medical-legal cases, but in order to continue, I needed to know more.

I am certain those two cases would have been my last cases with this attorney if I hadn't enrolled in Vickie's CLNC® Certification Program. He simply would have stopped using me, and I never would have known why.

I purchased the CLNC® Home-Study Certification Program and took Vickie's valuable advice. I quickly learned the value of contracts. In my excitement at the attorney's call, I accepted two assignments without a contract. I could have put in hours of hard work and never been paid. Vickie's program provided sample contracts I could easily modify for my needs.

Before becoming a Certified Legal Nurse Consultant[CM], I knew I had expertise in one nursing field, but Vickie showed me how to apply my expertise to a multitude of different types of cases. I would never have had the confidence to diversify or even thought to attempt it without her training.

The CLNC® Certification Program is so comprehensive, it's worth years of college education. I was never too tired to listen or study because Vickie's presentation makes the information interesting and relevant to my needs. The CLNC® Certification Program gave me all the tools I need to succeed as a CLNC® consultant. The sections on marketing, business development and report writing are worth the cost, not to mention the legal background essential for legal nurse consulting. I have never had a course with more useful information. Nothing is left to chance.

I am now confident in my ability to succeed as a full-time, self-employed CLNC® consultant. For now, I prefer to keep my job and consult part time. I plan to retire from nursing home investigation in five years. Thanks to Vickie's program, I know

"The CLNC® Certification Program is so comprehensive, it's worth years of college education."

how to market, and I'll have a significant client base established by the time I choose to retire.

Anyone taking the CLNC® Certification Program can quickly earn back its cost many times over, even working only a few extra hours a month. I did. I recommend taking the program *before* you start consulting to avoid making mistakes that could cost you money, clients and your reputation.

As my coworkers tried to tell me, the CLNC® Certification Program is an investment in my future, not an expense. I'm so excited about my success I want to share my enthusiasm.

Anyone taking the CLNC® Certification Program can quickly earn back its cost many times over, even working only a few extra hours a month. I did.

Vickie's Simple Networking Tips Paid Off Fast

by Sandra Broad, RN, CLNC, Florida

I can't believe it! Just three weeks after I completed Vickie's CLNC® 6-Day Certification Seminar, I'm off and running.

I want everyone to know that referrals and networking really do pay off. I followed Vickie's simple tips about networking and marketing, and I'm amazed at how quick and easy it was. I asked a friend if she knew any attorneys in the area, and she gave me a name. I went to see him and explained my CLNC® services.

Three days later he called to see if I would be interested in reviewing up to 200 cases a month from various emergency departments across the country for alleged medical injuries and billing accuracy. I jumped at the chance! What a great opportunity for my first assignment as a Certified Legal Nurse Consultant^{CM}.

I couldn't have done it without Vickie's marketing techniques and wonderful advice. Her CLNC® Certification Program truly is making all my dreams come true. A most heartfelt thank you to Vickie and her staff.

I followed Vickie's simple tips about networking and marketing, and I'm amazed at how quick and easy it was.

I Turned a Dull Career Path into Exciting CLNC® Rewards

by Jennifer S. Farney, RN, CLNC, Virginia

I am a fiercely independent risk taker always eager for the next venture. My full-time job as an occupational health nurse was taking me down a dull path and draining the excitement and joy out of my life. My boss informed me one day that I was a mouthy, opinionated rebel—and what was I going to do about it? Well, I agreed with him, took Vickie Milazzo Institute's CLNC® Certification Program and two months later turned in my resignation.

That took a great deal of faith, courage and risk. I have never looked back, only forward, and my ability to maneuver past obstacles and to concentrate on my strengths has gained the trust of many attorney-clients.

Two personal obstacles I face are raising a special needs daughter and watching my mother battle cancer. My personal obstacles came into my life long before I became a successful businesswoman, but my faith in God gave me the strength to overcome these trials. They have prepared me for future endeavors.

I currently consult full time with six law firms. My attorney-clients do much more than provide a paycheck. Most of the attorneys take additional time to thank me personally. They also challenge me to expand my knowledge as they give me more autonomy in managing their cases. I take pride in knowing my attorney-clients are referring me to their colleagues because of my excellent work product and work ethic.

I also take pride in networking and subcontracting with CLNC® colleagues. Together we reap the rewards of winning that difficult case. Together we encourage one another to grow both personally and professionally.

This year at the *NACLNC®* Conference I had another great adventure. Just three years after becoming a CLNC® consultant, I was a guest speaker at the conference lecturing on "How to Analyze Workers' Compensation Cases." What an awesome experience. I stand amazed at all I have accomplished as a successful CLNC® consultant.

I also have time to pursue my passion for medical missions. I have traveled to Panama, Russia and China, and this year I plan to travel to India. I love to share my knowledge with others around the world.

I will continue to expand my visions and passions and excel in life. As Vickie says, I am a Certified Legal Nurse Consultant^{CM} and I can do anything!

> *I take pride in knowing my attorney-clients are referring me to their colleagues because of my excellent work product and work ethic.*

My Success Is Written in the Stars

by Pam McDonald, RN, CLNC, Michigan

I attended Vickie's CLNC® 6-Day Certification Seminar with the clear intention of leaving hospital nursing and becoming a Certified Legal Nurse Consultant℠. My consulting practice already had a name, Aurora Consulting Services, for the aurora borealis. I can view the northern lights in my small, rural town as if I'm in a planetarium. I've always loved the night sky.

The moment Vickie stepped onto the stage at the CLNC® 6-Day Certification Seminar, she was a complete dynamo, and I immediately knew I would be successful. Vickie gave us the power to believe in ourselves, our nursing skills and experience, and our ability to become as successful as we want to be. Vickie and the Institute motivated me to get out of the hospital and start my own business. No more working holidays and night shifts for me.

My dream is already taking form. Although the small, tight-knit group of attorneys in my town don't litigate many medical cases, I started marketing to them. One attorney gave me a list of all the trial lawyers in Michigan. In addition to sending the usual resume and cover letter, I added that I specialize in OB. I also announced that I could present an in-service on fetal monitoring strips and would call in two weeks to ask how many would attend the presentation.

The moment Vickie stepped onto the stage at the 6-Day Seminar, she was a complete dynamo, and I immediately knew I would be successful.

Vickie motivated me to...start my own business. No more working holidays and night shifts for me.

One law firm consistently advertises in the local newspapers in my area. As it turns out, this attorney spends his summer vacation in my small town and has three other offices nearby. He grew up here, and we know many of the same people.

More important, he had a case for me to review. I went to see him, told him my fee and asked him to sign a contract. I walked out with a signed contract, $1,000.00 retainer and the medical records. I was thrilled, excited and terrified all at once. I called the Institute and a CLNC® Mentor guided me through my first case successfully.

Since then this attorney has given me two more cases. He told me he was pleased with my work and that I picked up things the MD missed, which really heightened my confidence. All my experience as a nurse was now paying off at $125/hr. I've worked on three cases for 19 hours and made $2,375.00.

My marketing efforts continue, and I have subscribed to our weekly lawyers' news publication which announces all the local and state meetings and conventions. This small publication has opened up a whole new world of marketing opportunities for me.

It is thrilling and exciting to work with attorneys who seek and truly value my professional opinions as a Certified Legal Nurse Consultant^{CM}. I'll meet my goal of leaving the hospital, and I will look out at the northern lights and realize that I made my dream come true with my hard work and the help of Vickie Milazzo and the Institute.

All my experience as a nurse was now paying off at $125/hr. I've worked on three cases for 19 hours and made $2,375.00.

It is thrilling and exciting to work with attorneys who seek and truly value my professional opinions as a Certified Legal Nurse Consultant^{CM}.

The CLNC® 6-Day Certification Seminar Made My Dream of Owning a Business a Reality

by Michele R. Groff, PHN, MSN, CLNC, California

Owning my own business had always been a goal of mine, although I did not know what shape would finally emerge. My experience in clinical nursing spans over 25 years, from Medicare hospices to home healthcare. In my last position as a director of home health and outpatient nursing services for a hospital system, I was exposed to medical records review and realized I could reach my goal as a Certified Legal Nurse Consultant℠.

I looked at the different programs available and even checked into several university programs, which were all paralegal-based. Then luckily, I saw an ad for Vickie's CLNC® Certification Program, which emphasized using my nursing experience and applying it to the field of law. This seemed to be a perfect fit for me. Since nursing has given me so much, I strongly agree with Vickie's perspective. As an advocate for RNs, she warns us not to fall into the role of paralegal.

I enrolled in the CLNC® 6-Day Certification Seminar and felt immediately connected. Anyone starting out in the field of legal nurse consulting needs Vickie's guidance, business savvy and valuable marketing tips. Vickie's CLNC® Mentoring Program has been critical to my success as a beginning CLNC® consultant. Purchasing all of Vickie's educational materials has also helped get my practice off the ground. I've used each and every one.

Vickie inspired me so much that I immediately quit my full-time position and started my own consulting practice. As an independent CLNC® consultant, I get to work on a variety of cases, and I also get to work as a testifying expert. I especially love the medical malpractice cases. Right now, I have 13 cases, and they all came to me by word of mouth.

"I have 13 cases, and they all came to me by word of mouth."

Referrals Multiplied Our
CLNC® Business Fast

by Sharon Moser, RN, CLNC and
Kathy Thompson, RN, CLNC, Ohio

After attending the CLNC® 6-Day Certification Seminar we told a physician friend what we had just accomplished. She immediately suggested contacting her husband, an attorney. The week after Vickie's program we had our first interview and left his office with two cases. Each time we turn in one case, we get another, sometimes two. The first attorney we worked with introduced us to another attorney, and we are now consulting on the biggest case that firm has ever had. In just three months we were able to quit our full-time positions at the hospital and continue nursing part time.

We have been so fortunate. The word-of-mouth referrals just keep coming in. We now work closely with three different attorneys. Each one has remarked how well prepared we are and what a good job we do. Just last week we received eight referrals because our clients want their colleagues to know about Certified Legal Nurse Consultants[CM]. "Attorneys really don't know about the medical issues in their cases," our attorney-clients say.

We have weekly meetings with attorneys from one firm to keep them updated on all the cases we are working on for them. The attorneys listen to us and value our opinions. It feels great!

Our cases are keeping us very busy, and we still have time to enjoy our lives. Most important, we are doing a job we feel proud of while helping others. We are our own bosses, and we learn something new every day. Vickie's CLNC® Certification Program was the step we needed to push us where we wanted to go. We should have done it years ago.

We believe our success is directly related to the CLNC® Certification Program. Vickie taught us the little things we would never have known, such as how to approach an attorney and how to market our services. She even includes sample letters to attorneys, which we used successfully. Other programs were available to us, but we chose Vickie's because she taught us everything we needed to succeed.

Thank you, Vickie, for being there, going first and sharing all.

Most important, we are doing a job we feel proud of while helping others. We are our own bosses, and we learn something new every day.

The CLNC® Certification Guaranteed My First Case

by Martha Bishop, RN, CLNC, Tennessee

Ns earn up to $150/hr." Who could pass up an opportunity like this? To a staff nurse earning less than $20/hr, this sounded intriguing, so I opened the large white envelope from Vickie Milazzo Institute and read on. I must have read the contents of that envelope four or five times.

Then I called some attorneys in my area and asked them if they were aware of Certified Legal Nurse Consultants℠ and the services they offer. Most were very enthusiastic when they learned of my interest in this career.

One of the attorneys, Mr. Brown, said that he would love to speak with me and asked when I could meet with him. This certainly was not what I expected to hear. I made an appointment, thanked him for his time and hung up. *Wow!* Now what?

My next thought was clothes. What on earth was I going to wear? My wardrobe consisted of jeans, T-shirts, scrubs and a few casual dresses. I called my best friend Marcie, a CPA, and told her what had happened. She graciously offered to loan me a business suit.

With the clothing issue resolved, I focused on the upcoming meeting. When the day finally arrived, I was nervously pumped and ready. I left my house an hour early to avoid being late. When Marcie called to inform me of a motor vehicle crash on the highway, I took an alternate route. So did everyone else. Then there was a wreck on the alternate route. I took a second alternate route, as did others. Despite all my efforts, I arrived ten minutes late for my meeting with Mr. Brown. What a way to make a first impression. Fortunately, he had heard of the traffic situation and understood.

Our meeting lasted almost 40 minutes. He asked about the legal nurse consulting program I planned to attend, and I told him I'd be taking Vickie Milazzo Institute's CLNC® 6-Day Certification Seminar in a couple of months. I explained that I wanted to help patients in a different venue (and the money sounded good too). He told me to come back to see him after I completed the Institute's CLNC® Certification Program and he would assign me a couple of cases and see what I did with them. *Wow,* again! I had cases waiting and hadn't even taken the CLNC® training yet.

The week of Vickie's seminar was amazing. After learning that I had passed the CLNC® Certification Exam, I called Mr. Brown as promised. We met again. Then he asked about my fees. Nervously, yet confidently, I replied, "$125 an hour." He said, "Okay," and handed me a case. On the

He told me to come back to see him after I completed the Institute's CLNC® Certification Program and he would assign me a couple of cases.

The week of Vickie's seminar was amazing.

way to my van, I thought, "*Wow!* I can do this. I can do anything!"

I screened the case for my new attorney-client. When I finished, I returned the medical record, along with my findings. I mailed him an invoice for my CLNC® services. A few weeks later, he mailed a check.

To celebrate my first case, Marcie and I spent four glorious days in Orlando, riding roller coasters (my husband doesn't ride them). I love roller coasters, the bigger and faster the better.

I have sat at the bedside of a patient dying of cancer. I have played "peek-a-boo" with a sick child in the hospital. I have held a patient's hand during a painful procedure. Now, I have helped a patient who had a meritorious legal case. As Vickie says, "I am a nurse and *I can do anything!*"

Triumph Over Any Personal Challenge

Shoulder Injuries Killed My Nursing Career—Vickie Brought It Back to Life

by Cheryl L. Bennett, RN, BSN, CLNC, Indiana

I'm a combat veteran—part of the Grenada invasion—with 30 years in nursing. You'd think I'd be immune to on-the-job injuries.

After leaving the military, I finished my federal career at the Department of Veterans' Affairs. I was also working PRN at a psych hospital. One night three patients assaulted me and injured my right shoulder. When that had almost healed, I returned to work at the VA hospital. In no way was I playing Super Nurse, as I'm prone to do, but while helping six other people lift a patient, I injured my left shoulder.

The only way to get my life back was to invest that money in myself and in a new future.

That second injury killed my nursing career as I knew it. Workers' comp settled for far less than I expected, even though I got the maximum amount. The only way to get my life back was to invest that money in myself and in a new future.

Over the years I had seen Vickie Milazzo Institute's advertisement in nursing journals and thought that someday I might like to become a Certified Legal Nurse Consultant℠. My shoulder injury made "someday" come sooner than I expected.

One Magic Pen Later–A Referral Kicked Off My CLNC® Career

Five months after attending the CLNC® 6-Day Certification Seminar, I received a promotional ballpoint pen—bright colors, my name, address and phone number printed on the side. It struck me that this was the only evidence of my being in business. I didn't even have business cards yet. I stuffed the pen in my purse.

A few days later I ran into a nurse I hadn't seen for quite a while. We chatted, and I told her about my new "career" as a Certified Legal Nurse Consultant℠. Embarrassed that I didn't have a business card, I gave her the pen. "Here's my phone number," I said. "We can get together and have lunch."

About two months after I gave away the "magic" pen, I got a call from a law firm. The attorney said, "You come highly recommended."

Highly recommended? I hadn't done a case yet. I asked if I could call back. I panicked about what to say.

"What Would Vickie Do Now?"
Inspired Me to Action

Frantically, I pulled out the *Core Curriculum for Legal Nurse Consulting*® textbook, thinking, "What would Vickie do?" Everything I needed was in that book.

Vickie said to always get a retainer. When I called the attorney back, I told him my hourly rate and that I required a $500.00 retainer before taking the case. He said, "No problem." At this point I still didn't know where he had gotten my name.

When I arrived at the attorney's office, the check was waiting. The attorney said, "I need you to locate an expert witness." I expected him to say he needed a nurse experienced in nursing home care, critical care or emergency. Instead, he said, "This is an excessive force case against the police department. I need someone trained in how to control people who are combative."

Was he serious? Yes. And he needed this person in 48 hours. "I can do it," I said, without a clue how I would manage.

He didn't seem at all worried. "The nurse who gave me your name said you can do anything."

Now I finally knew who had referred me, the nurse I'd given the pen to, the nurse I'd run into totally by accident. That proved to me what I'd learned in Vickie's seminar, that people know attorneys. All you have to do is tell enough people what you're doing and ask them to pass your name along.

> *I pulled out the* Core Curriculum for Legal Nurse Consulting® *textbook, thinking, 'What would Vickie do?' Everything I needed was in that book.*

> *I told him the hourly rate and that I required a $500.00 retainer before taking the case. He said, 'No problem.'*

Now the word is out. Every time I turn around, someone says, 'We hear you do such a good job. When can you consult with us?'

In only a year I've just about replaced my nursing salary—and I earned a very good salary.

I remembered that my sister-in-law has a degree in criminal justice. I called her. She said, "What you want is a certified instructor in defense tactics for disturbed behavior." She even knew a couple of people who qualified.

Then I remembered a nurse from the VA hospital. Her husband is a police officer who is certified and has won awards in using a baton to subdue. I called him and he agreed to be a witness.

Within 24 hours I had not one but three expert witnesses to fulfill my commitment to the attorney. He was so impressed, his response was, "I want you on my team."

Four Attorneys Keep Me Busy

Walking through my attorney-client's building, I recognized other attorneys. I'd seen them on the news being interviewed about their high-profile cases. One of these attorneys stopped by my client's office while I was there. Two days later, she called me. She had intended to use a nurse she knew on a case, but after hearing about me, had decided I was the better choice. I ended up with a big case on nursing home abuse.

Now the word is out. Every time I turn around, someone says, "We hear you do such a good job. When can you consult with us?"

I work with four attorneys, and that's keeping me busy. I can handle that many by managing my time well. In only a year I've just about replaced my nursing salary—and I earned a *very* good salary.

I'm amazed that I was so afraid of getting started. Vickie tells us exactly what to do—and it works. When I bumped into my friend and gave her that promotional pen with my phone number, without thinking I was following Vickie's advice, "Just do it." The nurse passed my name along with a terrific recommendation, and my career as a Certified Legal Nurse Consultant^CM snowballed.

None of this would have happened without the CLNC® training. When I was at the CLNC® 6-Day Certification Seminar, still suffering with chronic shoulder pain, Vickie's positive message came through loud and clear. Even with my traditional nursing career dead, I didn't have to sit at home moaning, "Poor me. My life is over." I owe my new life to Vickie, not only to her excellent training but also to the inspiration that comes from just being around her.

"I'm amazed that I was so afraid of getting started. Vickie tells us exactly what to do—and it works."

"I owe my new life to Vickie, not only to her excellent training but also to the inspiration that comes from just being around her."

I Earned $138,000 in Less Than 18 Months as a CLNC® Consultant

by Kathy G. Ferrell, RN, BSN, CLNC, Alabama

For ten years I was a nurse manager with a corporation to which I was dedicated. Then upper management changed, and the atmosphere became unbearable. My family and friends urged me to get out, but fear of change paralyzed me. My best friend had attended Vickie Milazzo's CLNC® 6-Day Certification Seminar, and she knew legal nurse consulting would fit me perfectly. For a year she urged me to attend—still I was too afraid to make the change.

In my position as nurse manager, I worked with the legal department regularly. I finally decided that knowing something about legal nurse consulting would benefit me in my current career, and I signed up for the 6-Day Seminar.

Vickie Opened a New Window for Me

Then without warning, I received an offer I could not refuse—resign or be terminated. In 28 years as a registered nurse, I had never experienced such a devastating blow. My heart hurt, my pride was wounded and my self-confidence all but died. I felt like I was crawling on the floor, struggling to find the strength to climb out a window. My salvation was that I had already registered for the CLNC® 6-Day Certification Seminar.

At the seminar one of the first things out of Vickie's mouth was, "We are nurses and we can do anything!®" How refreshing to hear that I was capable of doing anything. Vickie's enthusiasm was uplifting and contagious. Best of all, she was sincere. She had succeeded as a nurse and as a legal nurse consultant herself and had mentored many other nurses to CLNC® success.

In addition to Vickie's assurance that I could do it, I heard from other nurses who had met the challenge, succeeded and were willing to help me succeed. The CLNC® Certification Program was excellent and was presented in a way that kept me interested and even entertained. I had fun. I became determined to show Vickie and especially myself that I could be a successful Certified Legal Nurse Consultant℠. Sure enough, a new window was opened for me.

Vickie's Action Steps Are the Key to Freedom, Flexibility and Success

How did I do it? I went home, and every day I took one of Vickie's action steps toward my new career as a Certified Legal Nurse Consultant℠. I mailed my information packets and within a week I began calling for appointments. I bucked up my courage to keep knocking on those doors, because I was convinced I had knowledge and experience that could benefit the attorneys.

> *One attorney called me back after receiving my packet and said, 'I need help. I'm drowning!' Just four months after I became a CLNC® consultant, I received my first four cases from him.*

In my first year as a CLNC® consultant I made more than $68,000 from eight very respectable attorney-clients. In the next six months, I made another $70,000.

Several of those initial contacts eventually became clients. One attorney called me back after receiving my packet and said, "I need help. I'm drowning!" Just four months after I became a CLNC® consultant, I received my first four cases from him and made a good friend in the process.

In my first year as a CLNC® consultant I made more than $68,000 from eight very respectable attorney-clients. In the next six months, I made another $70,000.

Best of all, I have the flexibility to spend more time with my husband (and business manager), my children and my hobbies. The freedom that being a Certified Legal Nurse Consultant℠ affords is unsurpassed. I offer my sincere thanks to Vickie and all the dedicated staff at Vickie Milazzo Institute for helping me become a successful CLNC® consultant. I am a nurse and I can do anything!

How I Survived Downsizing and Divorce to Triumph as a CLNC® Consultant

by Dale Barnes, RN, MSN, PHN, CLNC, California

Seven years ago, I was director of home care, home infusion, hospice and lifeline emergency services at a well-known hospital, a prestigious job with excellent salary and benefits. The work was challenging and fun, and I really enjoyed my coworkers, both administrative colleagues and my staff. I had built a cohesive team, doubled my department's revenues, decreased costs and implemented many new systems. I was proud of becoming a businesswoman while remaining a nurse, and I was on a "high."

However, the hospital hired a new CEO who had very different plans. My job was eliminated, and they hired a businesswoman to run the department. She had no idea about the staff's nursing and clinical needs. Two years later, they realized their mistake and hired a clinical person for the position.

Meanwhile, I found a similar job as head of a hospital department for all home-care related services. This job presented two major challenges: the department had no computer system, and the employees were unionized. Just as things began coming together, the hospital was sold to a large corporation. Within two months, my department was closed, and all employees received severance packages and were sent on their way.

I was the victim of downsizing yet again. As if these career catastrophes weren't enough, four-and-a-half years ago, I got divorced for the second time.

What was I to do? Here I was, divorced, jobless and not wanting to go through another downsizing episode. My severance package would not last forever, and being dependant on my ex-husband did not appeal to me.

For a long time I had been receiving information about Vickie's CLNC® Certification Program. It sounded interesting, but I hadn't had time to pursue it. Now I pulled out one of those flyers, called for more information–and felt I had found my answer.

Determination Paved the Way to CLNC® Certification

Many years ago, I owned my own home-care agencies. I liked being my own boss. I had good business sense and people skills, and I enjoyed a challenge. My background was in oncology, then home health and hospice. I had my master's in psych and had worked in that arena for a while. I knew such an eclectic background would serve me well as a Certified Legal Nurse Consultant℃ᴹ, but I needed to earn money while building my CLNC® business.

I called on a friend in the home health field, the nursing director of a home infusion company. He said he needed another field nurse, and I jumped at the chance, knowing that as a per diem employee I would

My first case came from a friend who practices estate law.... This case brought more referrals.

have a lot of flexibility. I loved working with the patients and could work as little or as much as I chose.

I ordered Vickie's CLNC® Home-Study Certification Program. I watched portions of the program almost every day. I was sure I'd be able to finish the course, study and take the exam in six months. But life has a funny way of throwing us curve balls.

On my 50th birthday, I boasted that I did not feel 50. Nine years earlier I had an inoperable, non-malignant brain tumor. I had an annual MRI to ensure the tumor had not moved or grown, and I felt well and healthy. But two weeks after my 50th birthday I got very sick. I had some strange auto-immune symptoms and was left with no hearing in my right ear and unsteady balance. I was told the 8th cranial nerve had been permanently destroyed, but that the problem was unrelated to my brain lesion. I was unable to ascertain from which direction sound was coming. That problem remains with me, but I have learned to compensate.

The most annoying and frustrating result was that I couldn't study the CLNC® Certification Program for a few months. I felt a sense of urgency about completing the necessary work. Finally, I finished the program and passed the CLNC® Certification Exam.

I Contacted Attorneys Every Day

I was anxious to get started and decided to be a little aggressive. First, I contacted attorneys I knew, regardless of their specialty, and asked for

I got a call from an attorney... He desperately needed the services of a CLNC® consultant... I was in his office within two hours and walked out with a personal injury case... This attorney became a good client and gave my name to several colleagues.

referrals. My attorney friends were intrigued by what I was doing.

I made phone calls every day. I put together a packet of information to send to new contacts. My first case came from a friend who practices estate law. She had me go with her to a hospital to help assess a terminal patient so she could write a bedside will. I addressed the client's competency to make decisions based on physical condition, mental status and any medication effects. This case brought more referrals from the estate attorney.

Another friend who practices labor law had no work for me himself, but passed out my flyers at a meeting of plaintiff attorneys. The next morning, I got a call from an attorney who had picked up a flyer. He desperately needed the services of a CLNC® consultant and asked how soon I could come to see him. I was in his office within two hours and walked out with a personal injury case related to a motor vehicle accident. This attorney became a good client and gave my name to several colleagues.

Interestingly enough, most of my attorney-clients had either plodded through the medical records or hired physicians. Many of them wanted to know why I thought I could do a better job than they could. They believed that because they had been doing it for so many years themselves, they really understood the medical issues. Fortunately, I was able to show them that they did need me, and that using my expertise was more cost-effective than doing it themselves.

A couple of my best clients said they wanted to use me on every medical-related case. This was a good break for me, but unfortunately, these clients were not getting dozens of such cases every week. So I continued to work my day job.

My Marketing Efforts Paid Off Big

I joined three different networking groups and attended meetings religiously. After a while other members get to know you, understand what you do and become confident in giving you referrals. Most referrals from these groups came not from the attorneys in the group, but from attorneys other members knew and had me contact. I also started sending out an information newsletter every other month.

My efforts started paying off. Before I knew it, attorneys I did not know or contact were calling me. Attorneys for whom I worked were giving my name to other attorneys. I also gained three steady clients from my newsletters, a good response, given that my mailing was only going to about 400 attorneys at the time.

One of these steady clients is an attorney who specializes in dog bites and manages cases from coast to coast. I get 10-12 of these cases per month, from simple cases to those involving disfiguring injuries. I summarize the medical records for each case and provide the attorney a 1-2 page overview describing the injuries, treatment and possible future treatment. I charge for my time spent tracking and reviewing the cases and writing the reports.

My efforts started paying off. Before I knew it, attorneys I did not know or contact were calling me.

This client provides me with steady income every single month, and the work is the easiest I do. I have other steady clients, but their assignments are more complex. The combination is exciting and challenging.

Referrals Kept My CLNC® Business Flowing

Last year I moved from Los Angeles to San Diego. About six months before the move, I asked an attorney friend in L.A. if he knew any San Diego attorneys. He came up with several association lists of both plaintiff and defense attorneys. I made numerous phone calls and set up appointments with as many of these potential clients as I could. I always used my friend's name, stating that he had referred me and given me their number. Although he only knew a few of them personally, no one came right out and said they had never heard of him.

From these contacts came a multitude of new clients. One attorney actually handed me medical records as I left his office after our first meeting. Another attorney asked me to speak to his firm about the CLNC® services I could provide on bad-faith insurance cases. Another contact referred me to his buddy in the San Diego city attorney's office, who became a client.

Word of mouth was again a plus for me. After I had lived in San Diego for only three weeks, 40% of my client base was here. Referrals have helped my San Diego clientele grow. I have already received inquiries and requests for my CLNC® ser-

From these contacts came a multitude of new clients. One attorney actually handed me medical records as I left his office after our first meeting.

vices from attorneys who heard about me through other attorneys. I stressed to my Los Angeles clients (still 60% of my client base) that their cases will continue to receive the same quality service as when I lived in L.A. Email and FedEx® are wonderful.

I Made the Leap into a
Full-Time CLNC® Business

Despite these successes, until recently I continued to see home health patients for two agencies to earn "bread and butter" money. I always knew I could supplement my income with home health visits if the phone stopped ringing for a few days. In addition, my home health work gave me the clinical continuity to feel comfortable testifying about clinical issues.

At one of the *NACLNC®* Conferences, Vickie talked about taking that leap and letting go of secondary work in order to build your CLNC® practice into a full-time business. I really wanted to do this, but it was scary. After that conference I went home and told both home health agencies to call me only if they were really desperate for a nurse. Slowly, I weaned myself away and was able to tell them to take me off their rosters.

When attorneys ask about testifying, I tell them I will find a clinically active nurse to testify. I explain that although I still testify to the findings of medical record reviews, I no longer testify to clinical issues. This too was a leap, as my rate for testifying is double my consulting rate. I felt like I was letting go

What my CLNC® practice has brought me is total freedom. I feel emancipated. I no longer need the home health income; I have more than surpassed that.

of a lifeline, but I reminded myself that testifying to clinical issues was not the bulk of my business. Then I took the plunge anyway.

Sometimes I am so overwhelmed with work that I cannot complete it all in a timely manner. I then subcontract with other CLNC® consultants.

What my CLNC® business has brought me is total freedom. I feel emancipated. I no longer need the home health income; I have more than surpassed that. I don't have any desire to go back to a clinical setting. At times I do miss the patient contact, but I often get quite involved with the attorneys' clients. Many of them call me to ask for medical resources or nursing advice.

I feel like I have the best of all worlds. I am so happy Vickie encouraged me to step out of my comfort zone. I love what I am doing. I'm busy, challenged and financially secure, and I am so proud to be a Certified Legal Nurse ConsultantCM.

My Miracle Journey—From Park Bench to "Park Avenue"

by Denise C. Lemakos, RN, CLNC, New York

T wo years ago, I stood in the ambulatory care unit holding a dirty colonoscope. Case No. 6 canceled because the patient was noncompliant with her preparation. I glanced up at the light fixture filled with dead flies (where was maintenance?) and thought, "I can't do this anymore. I didn't get clean and sober for this!"

No one at the hospital knew that years ago I had survived a long history of neglect and addiction. I had been battered, homeless, living on the streets of Brooklyn for two years. After nine years of recovery the physical scars and bruises had faded.

I'd come such a long way, yet my career wasn't going anywhere. Every shift I endured eight hours of bickering among the five staff nurses I was assigned to work with. Even worse, my take-home pay was less than $14 an hour, pitiful for a seasoned operating room nurse with 22 years of experience. My heart told me I could be happy and do more with my life.

Then someone at work showed me a brochure from another nurse who had taken Vickie Milazzo Institute's CLNC® Certification Program. I thought, "I can do this."

I went to the Institute's website. With one little click I began a dramatic transformation in my professional and personal lives. The staff member who

> *I went to the Institute's website. With one little click I began a dramatic transformation in my professional and personal lives.*

Legal nurse consulting sounded so exciting, I signed up for the next CLNC® 6-Day Certification Seminar.

answered the Institute's 800-number explained a whole new venue for practicing nursing. Legal nurse consulting sounded so exciting, I signed up for the next CLNC® 6-Day Certification Seminar.

This was a daring feat for my family. We were already in major debt with virtually no money to spare. But my life on the streets paid off—I could take risks because I knew nothing worse could happen to me. I used "OPM" (other people's money), charging the course tuition, flight and hotel room. I wore borrowed business attire and ate cereal in my room at night to save on meals.

I was determined to continue on this new path, and I didn't let anyone or anything stop me. Nurses, doctors and some legal professionals tried to undermine my resolve. They told me there was no need for this service in my area. I proved them all wrong.

My Income Tripled as a CLNC® Consultant– and So Did My Time Off

In less than one year after receiving my CLNC® Certification, I almost tripled my income while at the same time tripling my time off.

In less than one year after receiving my CLNC® Certification, I almost tripled my income while at the same time tripling my time off. At 10:00am today, still in my PJs, with 31 inches of snow on the ground, I have already made $500.00.

One of my favorite assignments is sitting in on depositions. This is my chance to shine. When my attorney-client struggles to pronounce the medical terms, I pass him notes. Sometimes we can't help but laugh together. It's great having this valuable knowledge lawyers need to make their cases. I know more about what my attorney-client wants and needs than he does.

Recently, I had the glorious opportunity to attend an event where I hobnobbed with the New York State Bar Association LAP director, a former district attorney from a county near my home and about 100 attorneys and their families. I found my niche, and I felt comfortable with and supported by this group. I received three nursing home cases and two med-mal cases from this one weekend.

I love the challenge of creating a new freedom and a new happiness I never knew existed before. I also have the freedom to "give back" by participating in social service activities such as the state nurses' association peer assistance program.

The CLNC® Certification Program Set Me on a Lifetime Path to Honor, Dignity and Success

I am the proud mother of a 5-year-old son, and I have the time to go to his plays and other school activities. I take computer and business classes and attend writing seminars.

My husband is building me a beautiful office in our home. I picked the color pink because it's bright and happy, and I'll be spending a lot of time there reviewing cases. I'll also have my own website, thanks to a university program in which students build web pages for credit. My new career as a Certified Legal Nurse Consultant^CM is coming together,

> *I love the challenge of creating a new freedom and a new happiness I never knew existed before.*

just as Vickie said it would, along with my new image. I love dressing up in real clothes instead of constantly wearing scrubs. I go to a salon now to have my hair done, and I look like a woman again.

I'm not married to a hospital anymore, and my work is fun, interesting and lucrative. I call the shots, and I love not reporting to anyone. I dance all the way to the bank. The Mary Tyler Moore Show theme song said it just right: "We're gonna make it after all."

The Student Was Ready and the Teacher Appeared

Vickie Milazzo and her illustrious staff have put together an awesome program I can grow old with. At 46, I've done my share of being on call and working long hours with no lunch break, too many patients and a crabby staff. I can work as a Certified Legal Nurse Consultant^{CM} till I'm 80.

Sometimes I feel like Vickie is sitting on my shoulder. If I feel stuck, I hear her saying, "Just do it!" and it works. She empowered me to come out of my shell.

At one legal conference I attended, a presenter said, "If you can get a good legal nurse consultant, you'll be blessed." I went up and gave him my card, because Vickie's voice was in my ear, reminding me to network, network, network.

For years I lived through hell, often without enough money to buy a sandwich. Now, by the grace of God and Vickie Milazzo, I earn $125.00

I'm not married to a hospital anymore, and my work is fun, interesting and lucrative.

I call the shots, and I love not reporting to anyone. I dance all the way to the bank.

an hour. It's a miracle. I traveled a long, hard way from the streets, but only when I found Vickie's CLNC® Certification Program did I discover the path I was meant to take. The joy is in the journey. Today I am a woman of honor and dignity and a successful Certified Legal Nurse Consultant^CM.

> *I earn $125.00 an hour. It's a miracle.*

My CLNC® Career Gave Me a New Life for Myself and My Twins

by Lisa Panish, RN, MSN, ARNP-BC, CLNC, Florida

I attended the 6-Day Certification Seminar, and every minute was invaluable.

Within three months of becoming a CLNC® consultant, I had three attorney-clients.

"I love you one million peanut butter cups. That's a lot of love." My twin boys and I repeat that to each other every night before we go to bed. I know I'm lucky. What do you say about the most important people in your life? My five-year-old identical twins are the reason I became a Certified Legal Nurse Consultant℠—both have cerebral palsy and asthma.

I have been a single mom since my sons were 15 months old. As a healthcare provider, I have been blessed with opportunities that many others have not. I've been a nurse practitioner for almost ten years, and I have a wonderful job and colleagues. However, I was missing opportunities and therapies with my children. Sometimes I don't want to blink, because I don't want to miss anything in their lives.

As fulfilled and busy as my life is, my parents encouraged me to challenge myself more and try another opportunity. I learned about becoming a CLNC® consultant from my mother's nursing college roommate, who reported finding success and versatility in her new CLNC® career. Immediately after that conversation, the Vickie Milazzo Institute information packet arrived in my mailbox.

My parents and I discussed the opportunity to work from home, enjoy a flexible schedule and use my nursing skills in a different way. My parents are so helpful, but they want to enjoy their retirement. The more we heard about the Vickie Milazzo Institute CLNC® Certification Program, the more we all agreed that the CLNC® 6-Day Certification Seminar was a good investment.

Within 3 Months of Becoming a CLNC® Consultant, I Had 3 Attorney-Clients

I attended the 6-Day Certification Seminar, and every minute was invaluable. The wealth of information fascinated me, and I knew I had found a nursing profession I could excel in and enjoy.

I returned home full of motivation and ready to get started, but the responsibilities of a full-time job and sick children took priority. My friends knew I had taken Vickie's program and were excited for me. One girlfriend called to tell me that her neighbor, an attorney, was looking for a Certified Legal Nurse Consultant^{CM} to do some work for him.

And so my CLNC® career began. It all happened so quickly. My first case was the scariest, and I kept thinking, "Fake it till you make it." How many times did I hear that?

After that first case, my CLNC® colleagues began calling me when they were overloaded. I completed two more cases, and within three months I had three attorney-clients. My attorney-clients now refer me to their attorney colleagues—last week I received a call from a defense attorney.

> *My attorney-clients now refer me to their attorney colleagues—last week I received a call from a defense attorney.*

With the money I have made so far as a CLNC® consultant, I have been able to replace the tile and carpet throughout my home with hardwood floors. This change has made a difference in my boys' asthma and their mobility.

The learning curve has been huge, and the social atmosphere in the legal world is different from that in the hospitals, nursing homes and office practices where I have worked. On every case I am able to give the nursing perspective and add my personal experience as a nurse practitioner to strengthen the case. I look forward to challenging myself with other CLNC® opportunities and becoming more versatile. I want attorneys to see me as an asset and call on me because of my outstanding reputation in my new career.

With the money I have made so far as a CLNC® consultant, I have been able to replace the tile and carpet throughout my home with hardwood floors. This change has made a difference in my boys' asthma and their mobility. I have wanted to change the flooring since I moved in four years ago, but was never able to afford it until I became a CLNC® consultant.

I cannot thank Vickie Milazzo Institute enough for changing not only my life, but the lives of my special boys.

After a Life-Changing Illness, I'm Living the Confidence and Freedom of a Successful Certified Legal Nurse Consultant^{CM}

by Ann Wiseman, RN, CLNC, Maryland

> *I realized that as a Certified Legal Nurse Consultant^{CM}, I could continue to use my nursing experience and knowledge even from a wheelchair (what I saw as my future).*

Two years ago, I lost my job and my professional career. After being diagnosed and treated for rheumatoid arthritis for 18 months, I was losing mobility and dexterity, and had no idea why. Finally, I found that I did not have arthritis, but rather a severe cervical stenosis that was flattening my spinal cord. I couldn't even scratch my nose by myself, I was in terrible pain and I was facing the rest of my life in a wheelchair.

Today, I'm fully recovered. I'm respected and recognized in the community as a businessperson, and I'm treated as an equal by attorneys. I'm having the time of my life, and I'm finally able to visualize new dreams coming true.

I have God, my wonderful husband and a great surgeon to thank for my physical and emotional recovery. And I have Vickie Milazzo and the CLNC® Mentors to thank for changing my life. They gave me the education, support and encouragement I needed to attain goals I never thought I could dream, much less realize.

How Has My Life Changed?

I have the confidence to be who I am. Previously, I worked around the country as a traveling labor and

> *My fee is $150 per hour.*

> *The biggest change in my life since becoming a CLNC® consultant is having the freedom to live my dreams. Can you say 'bright red Mazda Miata'?*

delivery nurse. I enjoyed the work and the chance it gave me to be a "fly on the wall"—no relationships, no ties to the community and very few friends. That's the way I *thought* I wanted it.

After I married, I decided to try surgical nursing. I was working in the operating room as a circulating nurse when I found myself physically unable to do my job. I was losing my mobility, and I was literally losing my grip. I lost my job; I lost who I was. After losing my career, I started tossing my nursing journals in the trash as soon as they arrived. After all, I didn't need them anymore.

Just one month before my surgery, I kept a nursing magazine for some reason. That's where I learned about Vickie Milazzo Institute. After watching the *Preview Your New Life as a CLNC® Consultant* DVD, I realized that as a Certified Legal Nurse Consultant^CM, I could continue to use my nursing experience and knowledge even from a wheelchair (what I saw as my future).

By then, I had been out of work for six months and we were pretty short on money, but I applied for financing and signed up for the VIP CLNC® Success System. Six weeks later—the day after my six-week checkup with my surgeon—I was on a plane to Las Vegas to become a CLNC® consultant.

The CLNC® 6-Day Certification Seminar changed my life. Vickie and her staff gave me the confidence to learn who I wanted to be and then go for it.

I can talk to people and be a teacher. I always enjoyed helping people. I'd even thought about being a speaker and a teacher, but didn't have the confidence or the opportunity to realize those dreams until I became a Certified Legal Nurse Consultant℠. Starting with the exercise of saying "My fee is $150 per hour," I generated the ability to do even more. A year ago, I appeared on two local television interview programs promoting the CLNC® profession. As a result, I received the *NACLNC®*'s award for "Promoting the CLNC® Profession."

With my growing confidence I led a seminar for 25 attorneys at the Maryland Trial Lawyers Association (MTLA) headquarters and presented a college panel discussion with a judge and a trial attorney.

I can help my CLNC® peers and others. Because of my new-found confidence, I have a chance to give a boost to other new Certified Legal Nurse Consultants℠ by subcontracting with them. I also share marketing tips and encourage them with Vickie's mantra—"We are nurses and we can do anything!®" This is very rewarding to me. My CLNC® business and my confidence gave me the freedom to create, organize and chair my church's program to relocate refugees from Hurricane Katrina.

I finally have the freedom to dream. The biggest change in my life since becoming a CLNC® consultant is having the freedom to live my dreams. Can you say "bright red Mazda Miata"?

I work when and where I want; I go to bed and wake up when I want; I take a vacation or a day off to be with my family when I want. Most important, I have the freedom to find out who I want to be and then do it.

I work when and where I want; I go to bed and wake up when I want; I take a vacation or a day off to be with my family when I want.

Did I Have Obstacles to Overcome?

I'm not alone. This is the only business I know of that provides me with my own cheerleaders and experts—Vickie and the CLNC® Mentors.

Absolutely! Fortunately, I'm not alone. This is the only business I know of that provides me with my own cheerleaders and experts—Vickie and the CLNC® Mentors.

When I got home from the CLNC® 6-Day Certification Seminar, I started preparing my promotional packets for attorneys and news releases for the media. As soon as I found out I passed the CLNC® Certification Exam, I sent out my promotional materials. After receiving my news release, a TV station called and asked if they could interview me on one of their programs. I was scared to death. I was nervous about making mistakes, but I found that when you're passionate about something and when you know that what you're doing is right, it doesn't matter.

The first challenge I ran into was the need to correct attorneys' misperception that they had to work with a local Certified Legal Nurse Consultant™. I also had to inspire their confidence in using me. This was why I went on TV, spoke to professional and community groups and began a newsletter which is now received by 250 attorneys.

My biggest obstacle was believing that when an attorney was slow in responding, I was doing something wrong. That undermined my self-confidence until I learned that such delays were not "all about me."

For example, the first attorney I called wanted me to attend an IME for him and promised to call later in the month when he was ready. He never called and never responded to my letters or phone calls.

I was devastated and just knew I'd blown it. A few months later, I ran into him at the MTLA convention, and he said, "You know that IME I needed you for? You'll never believe this, but the client died, so I didn't need you after all." Learning that it's not about me has been my best and longest-lasting lesson ever.

What's My CLNC® Business Like Now?

During my first five months in business, I worked on getting a few good clients so I could develop experience and build my portfolio of quality work product. In my first year I handled 21 cases from 12 clients. The cases included medical malpractice, personal injury and criminal.

To get around the attorneys' gatekeepers, I discovered ways to meet attorneys away from their offices, such as by exhibiting, teaching a class for a legal association or writing for the MTLA newsletter. In addition, I periodically visit local law firms and bring fresh baked goods to the gatekeepers. We all know everyone loves treats.

In the last three months I've replaced my nursing salary through my CLNC® work. With my business increasing, I'm using CLNC® subcontractors more. Because I took the time early on to develop my work product standards, I'm able to maintain high quality and consistency in my signature product.

I achieved my success because I followed Vickie's wise advice. It isn't hard. Just add your enthusiasm and optimism to her formula, and you'll soon be living the life of your dreams with confidence and freedom. It works!

In the last three months I've replaced my nursing salary through my CLNC® work.

I followed Vickie's wise advice. It isn't hard and it works!

Feel the Beat of CLNC® Success– Then Get Out and Dance!

by Jan Boswell, RN, MSN, CLNC, Alabama

My partner and I have a motivational saying that hangs in both our offices. It defines success as getting out on the dance floor. Joyce and I have been successfully dancing the CLNC® dance for nearly two years. This is the story of our dance, both the upbeats and the downbeats.

I was a single mother of two when I started noticing the ads in nursing journals: "Earn $125-$150/hr." Wow! I called for the Vickie Milazzo Institute information packet, watched the free DVD: *Preview Your New Life as a CLNC® Consultant* and I was hooked.

The Freedom of Working from Home Was Music to My Ears

Until my divorce I had stayed home with my children, one of whom has severe learning disabilities. My kids were fast approaching their teenage years. They needed me at home. The possibility of being able to work from home and make good money as a Certified Legal Nurse Consultant^{CM} was music to my ears. Now I had to put my toe onto the dance floor. I admit I was scared.

I worked full-time float at the hospital. Many nights I got pulled to CICU where I worked with Joyce who was also thinking about becoming a

CLNC® consultant. We talked about becoming partners–she could dance the CLNC® dance with me.

I ordered the CLNC® Home-Study Certification Program. Although the material seemed challenging at first, I grew more excited with every module I finished. I took my CLNC® Certification Exam and passed! That was the first upbeat note of my CLNC® dance.

The month after I became a CLNC® consultant, Joyce took the CLNC® 6-Day Certification Seminar and also passed the CLNC® Exam. Our music was starting to play.

Our First Big Case Got Us onto the Dance Floor with a $12-Million Verdict

A few weeks after we started our CLNC® business, we received our first big case from one of the legends in the local law community. This helped us overcome all our fears. We had to do it. Our CLNC® services made a big contribution to the $12-million verdict our attorney-client won.

Even though we continued to work full-time at the hospital that first year, we earned $40,000 from our CLNC® business. While the music and the dance were often chaotic, we were having the time of our lives. We never missed a beat of the music. In one week we got eight cases. We just kept working on cases and making money.

So many people have helped me succeed. I always hear Vickie's voice in my head. The CLNC® Mentors are great.

Our Ever-Changing CLNC® Dance Keeps Our Successful Business Fun

Currently, we have three attorneys who consult with us regularly. We have consulted on medical malpractice, drug product liability and insurance fraud cases working for both plaintiff and defense attorneys. From case to case, the music changes and the dance is different–that's what makes our CLNC® business so much fun. I work from home and this makes a tremendous difference for me and my children–we love being together.

Joyce and I are both goal oriented. Our goal this year is to double or triple our income. We let nothing stop us. That's what it takes to succeed: persistence, faith and action. It's all about staying on the dance floor and dancing the dance.

Finding My Passion as a CLNC® Consultant Puts a Song in My Heart Every Day

So many people have helped me succeed. Joyce and I keep each other motivated. Of course, I always hear Vickie's voice in my head. The CLNC® Mentors are great, and the success stories of my CLNC® peers inspire me. But the people who help me the most are my kids. They have given up time with me and never complained. They applaud my successes and pull me through my missteps. They are the reason I am dancing the dance. They are the sweetest music in my life.

My CLNC® career has changed me and my life. I see a bright future for myself. The most important change is that I have found my passion. I am happiest when working on a case, calling a client or working on a new marketing strategy. I have a song in my heart all the time.

If you're wondering whether you can make it as a Certified Legal Nurse Consultant^{CM}, just put your toe on the dance floor, listen to the music and dance. You'll have the time of your life. I am!

You'll have the time of your life. I am!

I Love Going for It as a CLNC® Consultant

by Jeannie Shoeman, RN, BS, CLNC, Iowa

I have 15 years of psychiatric nursing in a county hospital, private hospital, group counseling and individual counseling, and I've worked every field of nursing. I had heard about Vickie and, over the years, I'd met nurses who had taken her CLNC® 6-Day Certification Seminar and become Certified Legal Nurse Consultants^CM.

I got my bachelor's degree and went to work for various insurance companies as a workers' comp medical case manager. Then I worked with managed care insurance for eight years until that company went bankrupt and I lost my job.

The insurance company had used nurses in marketing because people would listen to us. We could get our foot in the door, and I realized I was good at it, maybe because of all my years in psych and personal communication.

Working in the Insurance Field Sparked My Interest in the Law

Working in insurance, I became fascinated with the law. When my job ended, I got depressed and gained weight. I decided it was time to try legal nurse consulting, and I went to the *National Alliance of Certified Legal Nurse Consultants (NACLNC®)* Conference to find out more.

However, despite my successful track record in marketing for the insurance company, I discovered how different working for myself was. Making that first call to an attorney was hard. I looked at that long list of attorneys and felt daunted.

I remembered Vickie telling us we'd have to make several calls to get an appointment. I had to remind myself to be confident. At that point in my life confidence did not come easily. I had a lot of personal problems, including a death in the family. My adult son was seriously ill, and supporting him had drained my funds.

The one lead I got turned out to be a catastrophe. When I got the attorney on the phone, he said, "I have a client in Alaska committing suicide as we speak." I didn't have the nerve to follow up after that call ended.

Vickie Gave Me the Extra Kick to Start Calling Prospects

I was totally discouraged, but Vickie gave me that extra kick I needed. After the *NACLNC®* Conference, I took the CLNC® 6-Day Certification Seminar and left the training feeling empowered and full of energy. I now looked at that intimidating list of law firms and decided, "Why shouldn't I go after the really big ones?" I picked out the top ten firms and made the calls.

A woman at the office of a medical malpractice defense attorney said, "Our senior founding partner has thought about hiring a legal nurse consultant. I want you to leave him a personal voice mail."

> *Vickie gave me that extra kick I needed.... I took the CLNC® 6-Day Certification Seminar and left the training feeling empowered and full of energy.*

After a week he called me back. He asked about my resume. My one reference was an attorney who had recently been appointed judge. My prospect said, "I've known Bill for years. Why don't you send me your packet?"

When I met with the attorney, he seemed excited, taking me around and introducing me to the other 11 partners and the entire staff. He bragged about my wonderful qualifications and said he planned to hire me as a consultant.

My First Case Was a Win for the Attorney and Me

After the meeting nothing happened. I waited three months, thinking he wasn't interested after all. Then he called with the first case. Later, I learned it had taken him that long to get the records.

I had never done medical malpractice or worked for the defense. My experience was with workers' comp and personal injury. This was an involved case, and I was afraid I couldn't do it justice. I told my attorney-client I had an extensive network of CLNC® consultants and could find him a nurse who specialized in that area. However, he wanted me, nobody else. He saw something in me that I didn't. As a result, we both were winners. He won the case, settling for a lot more money because of information I found in the chart, and I won repeat business.

Since then I've completed six more cases for him. I worked up the last one from inception, billing for 60-plus hours. The checks I received were amazing—$2,500.00, $5,000.00, $6,000.00—for not that many hours of work.

Vickie's Training Helped Build My Confidence and Discipline

Even though I landed a big firm with those first calls, I still procrastinate doing the marketing. This year, at the *NACLNC*® Conference, a speaker talked about taking one step a day, even if it's a small one. Vickie's impeccable image also impressed me—it has such punch. I'm still working on building my confidence, and I realize now that looking good and taking that one step every day make me feel more confident.

Using the valuable tips from the *NACLNC*® Conference to build my confidence and discipline, I know I will succeed even more. I believe you have to aim for the top, go for the big one, just like I did when I landed that first top-ten law firm. I love going for it as a Certified Legal Nurse Consultant℠.

We both were winners. He won the case, settling for a lot more money because of information I found in the chart, and I won repeat business.

The checks I received were amazing—$2,500.00, $5,000.00, $6,000.00—for not that many hours of work.

Finding My Own Way

by Fredda Thomson,
RN, CLNC, South Carolina

Although I have been a CLNC® consultant for less than a year, I have felt that deep, gratifying feeling I can only describe as success. Success can be measured in many ways, and while my business is growing financially, my more important successes have been focused on renewing my excitement for my nursing career and helping others in difficult situations along the way.

After more than 34 years in clinical nursing I had become very disillusioned with my career, to put it mildly. Patient care and safety had dropped to a new low, while nurses were burdened with increased paperwork, more and sicker patients, fewer staff members, less autonomy in decision-making, as well as lower salaries and benefits. I had tried several different aspects of nursing, seeking fulfillment in my work once again. But I still dreaded getting up and going into work.

Why stay in nursing? Even a bad situation can become comfortable, especially when you depend on that paycheck every two weeks. The pattern is difficult to break. However, after 34 years, it was time for me to break that pattern. Several personal hardships helped me make that decision.

Personal Hardships Signaled Time for Change

Shortly after midnight on New Year's Eve, my daughter, Cinda, eight months pregnant with her second child, became ill with nausea and constant abdominal pain, unlike labor contractions. Her OB service admitted her to the hospital, where she was diagnosed as being dehydrated. She was treated with IV fluids and nausea medication, and discharged on New Year's Day. A nurse practitioner told her the symptoms were normal. But the pain did not go away, and after a week in agony with no food or sleep, Cinda couldn't take it any longer.

Her OB physician reluctantly sent her back to the hospital. The nurses who examined her said she needed an emergency C-section. The baby was breech and in trouble. The cord was beginning to separate from the placenta. With an emergency C-section, she delivered a beautiful 6-pound 6-ounce baby boy.

When I saw Cinda after delivery, I was surprised to see that her abdomen was still quite large, as if she were still pregnant. She was told that was normal after the second baby. The severe pain continued, but was controlled with medication, and she was discharged ten days later with a Foley catheter in place. The next day, when I saw my daughter, I truly believed she was dying. She could hardly lift her head off the pillow, and she was vomiting bile and hallucinating. I took her back to the OB doctor, and the minute he saw her, he knew something was gravely wrong. Cinda's blood pressure had

"I chose Vickie's CLNC® 6-Day Certification Seminar because it met my needs— I wanted the best, quickest, most credible, most cost-effective training."

dropped dangerously low, and an ambulance was called to rush her to the ER.

Cinda's appendix had ruptured—shattered actually. The surgeon had difficulty even finding it as bits and pieces were way out of place. Her body was filled with more than 1800cc of pus causing sepsis throughout her system, and the surgeon gave her a 50-50 chance of surviving the next few hours.

Over 3½ weeks Cinda had a total of five surgeries. She remained in the ICU on a ventilator in an induced coma because of the severe pain and ordeal her body was going through. The sepsis had affected every organ and system. Her surgeon was always totally honest with us, but gave us hope. Cinda "woke up" on January 30 and, a few days later, was well enough to be transferred to a regular floor where she remained for ten more days.

During those days and nights in the ICU waiting room I had ample time to think. I knew I needed to make some changes in my life, and I committed to doing so. The hospital where I worked was very supportive in the beginning of Cinda's illness. However, as time passed they became insistent that I return to work. I had to use my vacation time to be with her in the hospital, and even though I had time left I had to return to work shortly after Cinda was discharged. She could not even take care of herself, much less her infant son and daughter. Her aunt came to live with her for two months, and when I was not working, I was with them.

Once again, I got into a rut and my commitment to change was put on hold. Things were awful at work. We merged with another hospital and went through many changes. Everyone was walking on eggshells, and we were told more than once not to ask questions, just to do as we were told.

My final decision to leave clinical nursing came on Sunday, July 25, when I was assaulted and severely beaten by a patient. This time I heard the message loud and clear. As I lay in the ER that night, once again I had time to think. As I healed in the days that followed, it became clear to me that I did not want to return to clinical nursing. I decided to take early retirement. In my mind, I was finished with nursing. I did not know what I was going to do, but certainly not nursing.

Becoming a CLNC® Consultant Renewed My Career Excitement

While my early retirement was being processed, I happened to pick up a nursing publication and saw several ads for legal nurse consulting. I wondered for a few seconds what that might entail, then thought to myself, "What do you care? You're done with nursing!" But this time I listened and this time I acted. I looked into four training programs and I chose Vickie's CLNC® 6-Day Certification Seminar because it met my needs—I wanted the best, quickest, most credible, most cost-effective training.

I am not a risk taker, and I was very frightened about having to learn so much so quickly. The CLNC® 6-Day Certification Seminar changed my life. How I wish I had discovered legal nurse consulting many years ago. Becoming a CLNC® consultant

The feeling of helping others who may have experienced the same pain I had or, better yet, of preventing others from feeling this pain, is a large part of my success.

> *Vickie's CLNC® Certification has given me the ability to form my own company and make decisions based on my own needs, with a feeling of worth I have not experienced in any other nursing job.*

has brought excitement back to my career. The feeling of helping others who may have experienced the same pain I had or, better yet, of preventing others from feeling this pain, is a large part of my success. Vickie's CLNC® Certification has given me the ability to form my own company and make decisions based on my own needs, with a feeling of worth I have not experienced in any other nursing job.

A Life-Altering Twist of Fate Inspired My New Passion

by Jane A. Hurst,
RN, CLNC, Ohio

I studied the whole CLNC® Certification Program. It gave me the confidence to see that I already had all the skills necessary to be a CLNC® consultant— I just needed Vickie to show me the way.

I consider myself Vickie Milazzo Institute's "poster child." My life-altering journey to becoming a successful CLNC® consultant has had its share of ups and downs, and I owe the upswings to Vickie.

I was working as an instructor in an LPN program. I loved my work teaching students about body mechanics. Then I injured myself lifting my dog into the car. I ended up having surgery to repair a herniated disc. A few days postop I began experiencing a new, much more severe pain, yet I couldn't convince the surgeon something wasn't right. He told me I was expecting too much of myself. By the time I was finally admitted to the hospital for additional treatment, complex spinal infections had virtually destroyed two vertebrae, and I also had an epidural abscess.

I knew in my heart I was a victim of malpractice. My career in active clinical nursing was over. I decided to pursue legal action. The attorneys I chose were very good to work with, but they didn't fully understand my clinical picture. They even told me they weren't sure my case would be successful. I felt strongly that because the surgeon wouldn't listen to me, I was paying the price for his poor judgment.

Fortunately, I remembered the Institute's advertisement in a nursing magazine. I decided that if I could learn about the role of a Certified Legal Nurse Consultant℠, I could prove my own case. So in 1992, I sent off for the CLNC® Home-Study Certification Program. I'll never forget the day that box arrived. I thought I might have bitten off more than I could chew, but I buckled down and studied the whole program. It gave me the confidence to see that I already had all the skills necessary to be a CLNC® consultant—I just needed Vickie to show me the way and redefine that knowledge.

My first case was my own. The lawsuit proceeded successfully, largely because I was able to find research to support my case. I became very involved in the entire process, going to every deposition and being deposed myself. The trial lasted two weeks, and the jury decided in my favor and awarded a large judgment.

I found that I liked what I was doing and set up my home office. Since my physical activity is limited, with my office at home I can lie down when I need to and work when I want to. I consult with the law firm that represented me, and I even got cases from one of the opposing attorneys who deposed me in the suit.

I asked the attorney I'd worked with for so long to write a letter of recommendation for me. Then I sent out my promotional packets. The response was great, and I now have new clients.

Back when I was so sick, I wondered what I would do. Nursing was important to me. Thank goodness I am able to use my nursing background in my CLNC® work. I now realize this is exactly what I was meant to do.

We all experience twists of fate in some form. Fortunately, when my fate took a turn, Vickie was there to guide me through. Her words of encouragement and her enthusiasm triggered my drive to pursue my new passion. I think of Vickie as the mighty oak tree, and we are all her little seedlings (or maybe little nuts!).

> *I think of Vickie as the mighty oak tree, and we are all her little seedlings (or maybe little nuts!).*

Trust Your Ability to Rise to the CLNC® Challenge

by Denise Heath-Graham, RN, CLNC, Maryland

Vickie taught me to pan for gold where there is none. I am very proud to be associated with her. She and Florence Nightingale ought to go down in history together as nursing icons.

In 1995 I became disabled because of a back injury. Vickie's CLNC® Certification Program has been a lifesaver. It allowed me the flexibility to create my own success while being disabled and a new mother.

I started teaching pre-hospital providers how to write legally defensible reports that would keep them out of trouble. Recently I sold a textbook for the pre-hospital provider, *The Missing Protocol—A Legally Defensible Report.* The first time I promoted my book, it sold out in just over an hour, and people from Alaska to Australia have contacted me about teaching for them.

A huge case against General Motors came from that book. I wanted to tell the attorneys to contact Vickie Milazzo because she is the expert. But Vickie taught me to rise to the challenge so I took the case, and I've been successful ever since.

Legal nurse consulting is now my primary focus. Vickie taught me to pan for gold where there is none. I am very proud to be associated with her. She and Florence Nightingale ought to go down in history together as nursing icons.

Angel Voices Everywhere

by Jan M. Skadberg,
RN, BSPA, CLNC, West Virginia

Remember how your mom bombarded you with cliches while you were growing up? "A stitch in time...You reap what you sow...Don't forget to put on clean underwear because you never know if you'll end up in the emergency room." I hate to say it, but as I become older and wiser, I find myself repeating these same cliches to others.

My mom had another saying she was fond of: "Trust those little messages from God. Angels won't steer you wrong." Once again, she was right, but I never thought I'd live to see it.

Time for a Change

The angels may need some help to let you know when it's time for a change. Three years ago I had a house built and moved my ailing father to be closer to me. My little girl lost a leg due to osteosarcoma and had every postop complication in the book. Talk about feeling overwhelmed.

Meanwhile, my work was the pits—hospital nursing just didn't fit into the life I needed to live. We all have horror stories about shift rotations, working holidays and weekends, last-minute schedule changes. And don't forget the head nurse from hell, who must spend hours every night developing policies and procedures that have you screaming in

I received the CLNC® Home-Study Certification Program. It was time to get cracking on a new vision.

despair at the Lady Clairol counter or running to the nearest pharmacist for a refill on your Prozac prescription.

That's when I started hearing from my human angels. One of my coworkers handed me an ad for a legal nurse consulting course and said, "You've always been fascinated by the law. This might be an avenue you'd like to pursue."

I got the message. That day I called Vickie Milazzo Institute for their brochure then ordered, and promptly received, the CLNC® Home-Study Certification Program. It was time to get cracking on a new vision. After several months I finished the course work, took the exam and became certified to "fake it till I make it" as a Certified Legal Nurse Consultant℠.

Calling All Angels

Next came my finances. I needed money—badly. As a nurse, have you ever felt that you give and give and give, wondering if you'll ever be thought of, or thanked, for all you do? This was the perfect time for another of Mom's cliches: "You reap what you sow."

Prospectus in hand, I went to my local bank, ruing the fact that my 24-hour deodorant had given out in less than 30 minutes. But after the social chitchat was over, the gentleman said, "The loan is yours."

My mouth dropped. I hadn't even given him my cost projections. With a twinkle in his eye, he said, "You took care of my granddaughter nine years

I've worked my buns off. But everything has flowed smoothly and fallen into place almost effortlessly.

ago. Your work ethic is good enough for me." Thus I reaped what I'd sown and received my loan.

Angels now started coming out with a vengeance. My nephew and sister created my brochure and Web page (professionally, I might add), thus saving me oodles of resources and time. Another angel, in the guise of my godchildren's grandfather (who just happened to be in town for the holidays), rewired my house to handle my phones and computer, all to the lovely tune of $15.

Somehow, the parents of many of my NICU babies found out about my new venture. One new mother set me up with a fashion consultant. Four hours later I walked out of Nordstrom's feeling like a million bucks—and I received her hefty employee discount to boot. The lawyer-parents of several of my babies gave me the names of reputable attorneys. Other friends have shared computer knowledge or their time in their areas of expertise.

Every single one of my needs has been met. Don't get me wrong, I've worked my buns off. But everything has flowed smoothly and fallen into place almost effortlessly.

Mom Was Right

A funny thing happened on the way to my new CLNC® career. I rediscovered myself. My goals, values, priorities. My life. Thank you, Vickie, not only for your obvious dedication to the quality of your program, but also for opening the door to a greater understanding of my belief system. And for helping me finally realize that I am how and what I think.

A funny thing happened on the way to my new CLNC® career. I rediscovered myself. My goals, values, priorities. My life.

So where am I now? I've taken my first case and my goal is to be out of the hospital setting within the next six months. My father is thriving and has been a great asset in helping me start my business, and my little girl, who was given one to four months to live, is now active and well nine months later.

Sometimes RNs have the illusion that we have all the answers and never need help. My most humbling experience was to gratefully accept assistance from friends, acquaintances and strangers.

The greatest lesson I've learned from this journey, though, has been gratitude. It's easy to be grateful when things are going well. The greater challenge is being grateful for the difficult times and the process of working through those difficulties. And it's all up to me.

Yes, Mom, you *were* right. I have reaped what I've sown. It did pay to listen to those small, quiet angel messages. How grateful I am to have felt this outpouring of love and support. I am definitely blessed—and prepared.

Thanks, Mom. And thank you, Vickie Milazzo.

Make More Than a Living, Make a Difference

I Set Myself Free by Becoming a Certified Legal Nurse Consultant™

by Judia Sarich, RN, BSN, CLNC, Texas

Twenty-six months ago I was a burned-out nurse administrator. After working 80+ hours a week for more than five years, I had reached a point of severe sleep deprivation and I was facing potentially serious health issues. I needed to take action. After seeing Vickie Milazzo Institute in every nursing journal, I did.

Becoming a Certified Legal Nurse Consultant™ was not an overnight decision. I prayed for guidance and God sent the answer, but I wanted to make sure. I spent a year checking it out. I laugh about that now because I later learned that Vickie's CLNC® Certification Program wasn't costly at all.

Most other new businesses far exceed the start-up cost of becoming a CLNC® consultant, and other businesses don't include the quality training or the ongoing free support by CLNC® Mentors.

Fourteen months ago I became a Certified Legal Nurse Consultant^CM. I love what I do now. More important, I am confident my company's current success is built on a solid foundation and is positioned for dramatic future growth. Why? Because I'm using the building tools Vickie gave me.

I often hear Vickie say, "Write down a detailed vision of your business. Take one action step for your business every day. Use the free support of your CLNC® Mentors. Be creative. Make a commitment to your business." These golden mantras are the cornerstones of my success.

I Carved a Detailed Vision of My CLNC® Future

When I came home from the CLNC® 6-Day Certification Seminar, I was filled with excitement and determination, but I was at risk of losing all momentum that first week. I had a bad upper respiratory infection. I was so miserable I could have chosen to stay in bed heavily medicated.

Instead, the first thing I did—in between coughing, sneezing and wheezing—was take Vickie's advice: "Write the vision of your company." Vickie's voice was in my head. I wrote, took my antibiotics, used my inhaler, slept, woke up and wrote some more. Despite feeling awful, I built my future CLNC® success, gaining a clear focus on what it would look like. As Antoine de Saint-Exupéry wrote in *The Little Prince,* "A rock pile ceases to be a rock pile the moment a single man contemplates it, bearing within him the image of a cathedral."

This exercise allowed me to see where I was going. Patterning Michelangelo, I saw the angel in the marble and carved until I set him free. The only difference was that, in writing the vision of my company, I set *myself* free.

Starting Small, I Found Myself Accomplishing Big

Vickie's next cornerstone, "Take one action step for your business every day," became the most important building block of all. This mantra, lodged in my head during the CLNC® 6-Day Certification Seminar, has carried me through periods when I felt down and worried and through periods when my business was thriving so well I thought I could skip a day. I'm sure Vickie would agree with Zen master Takuan: "This day will not come again. Each minute is worth a priceless gem."

I don't care how big or how small the task is, I take action on my business every day. Some days I talk about my business to someone new, make one new contact call or brainstorm a new marketing strategy. Other days I send a thank-you note or re-organize my office for efficiency.

The power of taking daily action for your business is immense. Many days I didn't feel like doing

> *I don't care how big or how small the task is, I take action on my business every day.... The payoffs have been great.*

anything, but I went into the office to do that one
thing and by the end of the day I was amazed at
how much I had accomplished. The payoffs have
been great. All those single action steps are the peb-
bles that have built my business.

Free CLNC® Mentoring and the *NACLNC®* Association Are My Built-In Support System

Another building block Vickie offers is the
Institute's free support—the CLNC® Mentors,
NACLNC® network and online tools in the
NACLNC® Association. Not a week goes by that
I do not refer to one of the many materials in my
VIP CLNC® Success System. I have used each of
these great resources, and each one has played a
part in my company's success.

The Institute's CLNC® Mentors are supportive,
knowledgeable and helpful in every situation. As a
new CLNC® consultant making that first client call
or setting that first appointment, I found talking to
a seasoned CLNC® Mentor invaluable. But these
are the obvious times I needed them. Many times
the CLNC® Mentors have surpassed my expecta-
tions with great responses to unusual questions.

Our *NACLNC® Directory of Certified Legal Nurse
Consultants* is another indispensable resource. I have
had the opportunity to present several CLNC® peers
as testifying expert candidates. I have made a commitment to use only Certified Legal Nurse Consul-
tants^CM as nurse testifying experts.

I Now Have the Energy, Time and Ability to Help Others

The final building block is one of the strongest cornerstones of my business. Vickie and more than one of the faculty members at the 6-Day Seminar said, "Be committed to your business." To me this also means be committed to God and give something back to others. I became a nurse because I wanted to make a difference, and I felt I had lost this ability. Now as a CLNC® consultant, I have the energy, time and ability to help others. I am more available to my family, my neighbors, my church and my community. I have time to participate in a volunteer organization that helps a local home for the mentally challenged.

How different my life is today. I'm busy and my days are full, but balanced, not chaotic. I am in charge of my life and my business. My work environment is healthy. There's no traffic to fight, no unproductive meetings to attend. I love my home office work space and using technology to reach out to clients across the nation. I have attorney-clients in California, Utah, Wyoming and Texas.

I have found balance and fulfillment in my life again. Thanks to Vickie Milazzo, the visionary pioneer whose fearless leadership and willingness to share have made such an impact on me and thousands of other nurses, I am a successful Certified Legal Nurse Consultant℠. I'm proud to be a CLNC® consultant. As Vickie says, "We Are Nurses and We Can Do Anything!®"

"How different my life is today. I'm busy and my days are full, but balanced, not chaotic. I am in charge of my life and my business."

"I have attorney-clients in California, Utah, Wyoming and Texas."

This single attorney-client can keep me busy full time.

I wow them with the CLNC® services I can provide to help them win cases and they treat me as a professional.

Just 2 Months After I Became a Certified Legal Nurse Consultant I Landed My First Big Client

by Melanie V. Paquette, RN, BSN, CLNC, Texas

For the first two months, nothing was happening. What was I doing wrong?

My husband said, "Give it a chance, Melanie. Let me help."

He began calling the attorneys I had sent postcards to, and he got results. He booked me for presentations at law firms where I discovered that face-to-face interaction is my strong suit. Once an attorney agrees to a presentation, and I show what I can do, closing the sale is a given.

My first big client, however, came by way of a referral from my insurance agent. My agent's neighbor is an attorney who referred his medical malpractice and personal injury cases to another attorney. That's when I found out how useful it is to know people who know people who know people. He passed my name along, and I got a call.

"What can you do for us?" the attorney asked.

Boy, did I answer that question. Amazingly, their firm hadn't used legal nurse consultants. Their paralegal was pulling her hair out, unable to provide what they needed.

In closing I asked, "When may I come to your office and show you what I can do?"

The Work Started Flowing and We Replaced My Husband's Salary

I handle all of that attorney-client's cases, including medical malpractice, personal injury and workers' comp. This single attorney-client can keep me busy full time, but my goal is to grow big enough to hire CLNC® subcontractors. We're almost there. We have four attorney-clients now–and the work keeps flowing.

I say "we" now because my husband left his job and came to work for me full time as an office manager. That was one of the smartest moves I made. A disabled veteran, he's able to take care of our children and still help with our marketing. He also answers the phone, which means an attorney gets a live voice, not an answering machine.

Being responsive is one important reason our business has grown so fast. We make $5,000-$6,000 per month and have already replaced my husband's salary.

I Like Educating Attorneys–Once They Know You, They Need You

The most amazing thing happens when I give a presentation at a law firm: attorneys pay attention. I wow them with the CLNC® services I can provide to help them win cases and they treat me as a professional. I use their feedback to refine my presentation for the next time I deliver it.

After attorneys learn what a CLNC® consultant can do for them, they see the value. Later, when I actually work with them, they begin to rely on me

After attorneys learn what a CLNC® consultant can do for them, they see the value. They begin to rely on me in more and more areas, on more and more cases.

in more and more areas, on more and more cases. Just recently, our biggest attorney-client emailed us to say we had become their best friends and they cannot function without us.

Being a nurse is important to me, and my CLNC® business makes me happy in many ways I never expected.

One thing I learned from Vickie is to hold my ground on nonmeritorious cases. That principle is working for me. After I review a case, my client will ask, "Melanie, what's your recommendation? What do I do with this?"

If the case has merit, fine. I lay it out. But I sometimes have to say, "I understand that something bad happened, and your client is upset about it, but I don't see merit here." In the long run, the attorney saves money by not pursuing cases he can't win.

My attorney-clients listen to me and respect my judgment. That makes me feel that my nursing experience and knowledge are making a difference.

While taking my CLNC® training, I came up with the slogan we use in our marketing: *We make you look best.* My attorney-clients love it.

I Enjoy What I Do Every Day

Being a nurse is important to me, and my CLNC® business makes me happy in many ways I never expected. I enjoy my attorney-client relationships. I enjoy feeling that I'm still helping people, even though it isn't at the bedside.

On every case, I learn something new, which I can then use on future cases. That's exciting. While I'm teaching my attorney-clients about medical records and the healthcare side of a situation, they're handling the legal side and I'm learning from them, too. Together, we make a brilliant team. I help identify issues that will help them look good in the courtroom and win the cases that deserve to be won.

I also enjoy knowing that my children are not spending time at daycare. I used to feel guilty about leaving them, but now they're getting the best care at home with their father. My CLNC® business has positively impacted our entire family.

After serving his country in Iraq, my husband came home with limitations that make it hard for him to work outside the home. I created a job for him, and he's a valuable asset to my CLNC® business. No one could do a better job running the office, and I love working with him. This could never have happened if I'd stayed full time at the hospital. I'm proud that ours is a family business, that we can grow it together.

Recently, I've begun traveling for my attorney-clients, which is another exciting aspect of what I do. On one case, the attorney requested that I meet with his client who needed to be assessed for a life care plan. When I asked the attorney if he wanted me to find someone local to assess his client in order to save on travel cost, he insisted that I go myself because of the quality of my work. I was flattered. My office-manager husband made all the travel arrangements for me to fly in early one morning and come back the same day. This was a wonderful experience! I had never had a frequent flyer card before now. I feel professional!

> *My CLNC® business has positively impacted our entire family.*

We Keep Marketing Smart to Attract New Attorney-Clients Like Vickie Taught Us

One day we drove past a billboard for a law firm that specializes in personal injury cases. I told my husband, "We should call on them." He called and booked me for a presentation.

That's the sort of marketing that gets big results at low cost. This month we'll be mailing out and following up on a hundred postcards.

We offer a discount on the first case. Attorneys are like anybody else when it comes to saving money. The discount encourages them to take a chance, and it costs us nothing until a prospect actually hires us. We do a great job, the client is impressed and hires us again at our full rate. Marketing can be effective without draining your bank account – Vickie taught me that too.

Vickie Made It All Possible

I feel very lucky to have been trained by Vickie Milazzo. She's amazing. When I completed the CLNC® Certification Program, I told my husband, "Vickie's a tiny lady but powerful. She looks at you like you're the only person on the planet. The world around her stops and she listens to you, giving you her time and all her attention."

It has been a year now since my CLNC® Certification. A very happy year. I think back to those first two months, when I doubted myself, and I have to laugh. My life has changed in so many wonderful ways since I became a Certified Legal Nurse Consultant^CM.

I feel very lucky to have been trained by Vickie Milazzo. She's amazing.

My life has changed in so many wonderful ways since I became a Certified Legal Nurse Consultant^CM.

Success and Time with My Children Are Possible as a CLNC® Consultant

by Arnita Christie, RN, BSN, MS, CLNC, Connecticut

I transitioned from bedside clinical nursing into sales with the last eight years in pharmaceutical sales. But I always wanted to be independent and own my own business. I'd seen Vickie Milazzo Institute's advertisements in the nursing journals for many years, and I believed the CLNC® Certification Program would give me the chance to achieve my goal of owning my own business. I wanted to learn from the pioneer so I would be totally comfortable with the attorneys' language and my responsibilities as a CLNC® consultant.

I enrolled in the CLNC® 6-Day Certification Seminar and the 2-Day *NACLNC®* Apprenticeship. In the 6-Day Seminar, I received a great deal of information, and the 2-Day Apprenticeship put it all together and showed me how to market, interview with attorneys and write actual case reports. Receiving hands-on experience helped tremendously in activating my 90-day marketing plan. Within two months, I had my first case, a workers' compensation case.

With the CLNC® Marketing LaunchBox I Was Ready to Get Started on Day One

What helped me succeed was really listening when Vickie talked about developing a plan, writing

The 2-Day Apprenticeship put it all together and showed me how to market, interview with attorneys and write actual case reports. Within two months, I had my first case, a workers' compensation case.

down goals and taking an action step every day. I also prayed a lot.

When I returned home from the CLNC® 6-Day Certification Seminar, I looked at my 90-day marketing plan and said, "I need to do something every day." First, I sent out more than 150 emails to everyone I knew. I explained that I was a Certified Legal Nurse Consultant^CM and asked for attorney referrals. I received numerous responses, and I began working on those referrals.

My CLNC® Marketing LaunchBox materials were right there for me so I was able to begin marketing immediately. Not having to create and design my promotional package saved me many hours and thousands of dollars.

Next, I went online and researched the various attorney referrals I'd received. Then I did what Vickie taught me: I practiced in front of a mirror, I practiced in front of my kids and in front of my husband. I picked up that phone and I called the attorneys to request an interview. I ended up with a couple of phone conversations and four attorney appointments.

Vickie and the CLNC® Mentors Guide Me Every Step of the Way

With my CLNC® training and my nursing experience, I'm able to review and analyze a medical chart, and provide my attorney-clients not only with information about what's in the chart, but also with information about what's missing that they might not notice.

I absolutely recommend the CLNC® Certification Program to anyone even thinking about reviewing medical cases or working with attorneys. Vickie is magnetic and her words just grab you. She speaks from the heart–nurse-to-nurse. This program is designed specifically for us. You have to be a nurse to appreciate that. Vickie's education and the CLNC® Mentoring Program made launching my CLNC® business achievable for me.

Attorneys speak a different language than nurses. So I wanted a support system, and the Institute's program provides me with that. I use the CLNC® Mentors in all parts of my business, from my television interview to my first case, to any new hurdles. The CLNC® Mentors gave me suggestions about what to review before the TV interview and they have coached me on every aspect of my cases. I haven't taken a step without them. Having an energetic mentor like Vickie and the unlimited CLNC® Mentoring I receive as a VIP are priceless.

My next step will be offering my services as a speaker to the state bar association. I plan to inform the attorneys about new trends affecting their cases from the medical perspective and the resulting pitfalls their clients may face. This will give me a platform for describing my CLNC® services and showing how I can assist on their legal teams in dealing with these issues.

> *The best personal benefit of becoming a CLNC® consultant has been finding balance in my life.*

I Can Advocate for Patients and My Children at a New Level

One of the best things about my CLNC® business is helping. Even as a little girl, I wanted to help people. My mom said that if I saw a tattered doll, I'd try to fix it or put a Band-Aid® on it. That helping spirit is inside me. Now, I help people in a different way. As a bedside nurse, you're a patient advocate. As a CLNC® consultant, I'm able to support my attorney-clients while upholding the standards of care for nursing.

The best personal benefit of becoming a CLNC® consultant has been finding balance in my life. I'm the proud mother of two small children, and it is important to me to be active in their education and after-school programs. Working 50 to 60 hours a week, whether in nursing or in pharmaceutical sales, did not allow me to do that. When you have children, balance is essential–not just working all the time–because you cannot get back the years of their youth. Today, I'm a full-time Certified Legal Nurse Consultant^CM, and I'm able to participate in my children's lives. That's what having my own CLNC® business has provided me. Just as important as being there for my family, I can also help pay the mortgage.

Thank you, Vickie, for everything.

You'll Know It When You Find It— And I Found It!

by Suzi Sharp, RN, BSN, CLNC, Washington

I've been in nursing for 37 years, so I've done a zillion things—medical-surgical, pediatrics, OB/GYN, geriatrics, orthopedics, family practice, home health, hospice care, intravenous therapy and emergency care. I've lived and worked on an Indian reservation and even spent a month in Afghanistan.

I took early retirement, but after about a year I was ready to *do* something. Retirement stinks! I considered nursing jobs, but I didn't want to do that anymore. Plus, I didn't want to work for peanuts, and the stock market slump had eaten a large portion of my retirement nest egg. I wanted to do something I loved that would pay me what I'm worth.

One day, I told my eldest son, the "artist," that I didn't know what to do with myself. He said, "Mom, don't worry about it. Just lay back. It'll come to you and you'll know it when it comes."

Vickie's CLNC® Certification Program Cured My "Retirement Blues"

About that time I saw a colorful ad in a nursing publication. That's when I learned about Vickie Milazzo Institute's CLNC® Certification Program.

I didn't know much about legal nurse consulting, although I had been deposed and had testified

> *I took early retirement, but after about a year... I wanted to do something I loved that would pay me what I'm worth.*

as a witness a few times. My main connection with the law was my father. I grew up in a courtroom because my dad was an attorney, and he often took me with him. There wasn't anything better than going to court and watching him in action.

Vickie's ad about becoming a Certified Legal Nurse Consultant^CM fascinated me. I requested information and I checked out the Institute's website, all the while thinking, "This sounds too good to be true. What's the catch?" I talked to my other son, the "practical" stock broker, who said, "What do you have to lose?"

I still had some money stashed away so I went to the CLNC® 6-Day Certification Seminar. I loved the great professional training and I was so glad I did it. I was really excited when I learned I had become certified, because the CLNC® Exam was tough. In fact, I'm looking forward to attending the next *National Alliance of Certified Legal Nurse Consultants (NACLNC®)* Conference, because with Vickie there, I know I'll get pumped up, and there's no certification exam at the end.

A month after attending the 6-Day Seminar, I produced a business plan, had a logo designed and business cards printed. I developed my website and started advertising in a local attorney newspaper. I began marketing by calling attorneys, sending out information packets and following up on leads.

About that time, I was invited to go to Afghanistan for a month to help with medical services. I was thrilled and began preparing to leave the country.

Three Cases Started
My Success Snowball Rolling

A week before my departure, two attorneys called and wanted to hire me for their cases. Two days later a third attorney called. Fortunately, all of them (three attorneys in three different cities) agreed to wait for me to return from Afghanistan.

When I got back home, I started my CLNC® career in earnest with these three cases. One was a huge case for which I eventually reviewed more than a thousand pages of records and earned more than $10,000. I made a total of $25,000 in the next three months, and I was in business from then on.

Other attorneys are now discovering that I offer a valuable professional service. They know I'm thorough, reliable and trustworthy and I take my work seriously. The CLNC® Certification Program has really paid off. My legal nurse consulting business continues to grow.

My Nursing Know-How Makes
a Big Difference in My CLNC® Cases

As a Certified Legal Nurse Consultant^{CM}, you can generate work for yourself once you learn the medical circumstances of a case. For example, one of my attorney-clients represented a young Native American woman who lived on a reservation and whose medical situation was being judged unfairly. I looked more closely into her records and pointed out some medical issues the attorney hadn't consid-

> *I made $25,000 in the next three months, and I was in business from then on.... [Attorneys] know I'm thorough, reliable and trustworthy and I take my work seriously.*

ered. He told me to find an expert witness to testify to the special circumstances of the case. By following my nursing instincts and then asking pertinent questions, I shed a whole new light on the case and generated more business for myself. Most important, I pointed out extenuating medical conditions that warranted a larger financial settlement for the young woman.

A CLNC® consultant can make a big difference in a case. By citing medical aspects the attorneys hadn't noticed, I have just about handed them what they needed to win several cases.

For example, I worked for the defense on a major case involving a man's alleged sexual abuse of his daughter. The now-adult woman supposedly had childhood memories of the abuse. After poring over the records for 2½ months, seven days a week and most evenings, and reviewing about 1,000 pages of charts, I discovered she was a prescription drug addict and had told different stories about the alleged assaults to different counselors. In addition to my comprehensive report, I wrote a three-page summary of my findings. When my attorney-client read my summary, he asked, "Can you back up everything you've reported?" I said, "Of course." He exclaimed, "Holy cow! We've just won this case!" As a CLNC® consultant, sometimes you do more than provide direction on the case with your nursing experience—sometimes you have a major impact on the outcome.

I feel so good about what I do. I just love it. The cases are so much fun, so interesting and so challenging, I don't notice the clock. I can work at my own pace and there's no mandatory overtime.

Vickie's CLNC® Training Put Me on an Equal Footing with Attorneys

When I was getting ready to retire, I thought, "What a waste not to use the nursing knowledge and experience I've gained during the past 35 years." Now, I not only get to use my knowledge, but I can also increase it. When people ask what a Certified Legal Nurse Consultant^{CM} does, I usually tell them, Certified Legal Nurse Consultants^{CM}, get to sleuth through medical charts. It's like being a detective."

Vickie gives us the training and insight to deal with attorneys on an equal footing. She tells us repeatedly, "You will know how to do the job." And she's right. At first I felt lost, but then I remembered what Vickie says: Attorneys may be the masters of the law, but as a CLNC® consultant, I'm the master of the medical chart. As I followed her lead, I not only got the job done, but I also built a lot of self-confidence. I now know how necessary we as Certified Legal Nurse Consultants^{CM} are and how good we can be for a case.

Soon I'm meeting with a firm that has 40 personal injury attorneys. I'm going to walk in that door thinking, "Just give me a case and I'll show you what I can do."

I have tremendous admiration, respect and gratitude for Vickie. She is so genuine and passionate

> *I feel so good about what I do. I just love it. The cases are so much fun, so interesting and so challenging, I don't notice the clock. I can work at my own pace and there's no mandatory overtime.*

about helping nurses become CLNC® successes, and her enthusiasm motivates and inspires others. I also like the Institute's CLNC® Mentoring Program. The CLNC® Mentors always increase my knowledge. I just wish I had discovered Vickie's program sooner.

My son told me I'd know what to do with myself when I found it, and he was right. I've found myself as a CLNC® consultant, and I can do this until I'm 92!

Vickie gives us the training and insight to deal with attorneys on an equal footing.... Vickie says: Attorneys may be the masters of the law, but as a CLNC®, consultant I'm the master of the medical chart.

One Phone Call Mushroomed into My Full-Time CLNC® Business

by Susan Porter, RNC, BS, CLNC, South Carolina

I have 33 years of nursing experience in several different fields. A few years ago my husband saw an advertisement for Vickie Milazzo Institute in one of the nursing magazines and said I'd be good at legal nurse consulting.

We had recently adopted a special needs infant and it was three years before I could feel comfortable being away from home. Then I enrolled in the CLNC® 6-Day Certification Program and became a Certified Legal Nurse Consultant℠.

My husband, who's always my motivating factor, started sending out the promotional materials from my CLNC® Marketing LaunchBox to attorneys. He said, "You need to start answering your phone with Susan Porter and Associates."

Thanks to Vickie I Knew Exactly What to Say When the First Attorney Called

One week after my letters and brochures went out, I was taking my daughter to school when my phone rang. I answered "Susan Porter and Associates." The voice on the other end said, "This is Mary Sue. I'm an attorney. I received your CLNC® information packet and I have a home health case that I think you'd be perfect for."

> *Thanks to the CLNC® Certification Program, I knew exactly what to say so when the attorney asked what my fees were—I said $150.00 an hour. She said, "That's perfect."*

I had to pull over to the side of the road and take a deep breath—she was actually interviewing me on the phone. Thanks to the CLNC® Certification Program, I knew exactly what to say so when the attorney asked what my fees were—I said $150.00 an hour. She said, "That's perfect." We set up a meeting the following week, and in the meantime, she sent me the records to review.

When I went to her office, I learned that this was the largest defense firm in my hometown in South Carolina. The firm has five partners and 14 attorneys. I left with two more cases from their office, and another attorney from the firm soon called me on a new case.

After my first case, I cut back to one day every two weeks at the hospital. In just months my CLNC® practice mushroomed. A defense attorney who switched to plaintiff work asked me to continue reviewing his cases.

In one of the cases, the hospital involved was sold. A different law firm took over their case and asked me to send my final bill. I thought the case was dead for me, but the attorney who picked it up called from North Carolina and asked if he could meet with me. We met, and he asked me to continue reviewing the case, which settled two days before going to court. He also referred me to a colleague in North Carolina.

I just got another referral from an attorney in the original law firm whom I hadn't even met.

I Paid for My VIP CLNC® Success System in Two Cases

My CLNC® practice was mushrooming and I was exhilarated. It only took my first two cases to pay for the VIP CLNC® Success System.

I don't know how anybody could be a legal nurse consultant without taking the CLNC® Certification Program. Without it I would not have known what to do or where to begin. I still review the *Core Curriculum for Legal Nurse Consulting®* textbook with every case.

The CLNC® Mentors are invaluable. I had so many things to ask and I wanted to make sure I was on the right track. The CLNC® Mentors are always there to help, and every question is handled professionally.

I also attended the 2-Day *NACLNC®* Apprenticeship, where I learned to apply the principles in the CLNC® Certification Program and the *Core Curriculum.* The Apprenticeship gave me the skills to think on my feet with attorneys. Role playing was especially helpful. I was able to see a case in action and experience what it would be like before I went home and tried it myself.

Staying Visible to the Attorneys Keeps Me Successful

From the time I received that first phone call, I made a point of being visible to the attorneys, like

My CLNC® practice was mushrooming and I was exhilarated. It only took my first two cases to pay for the VIP CLNC® Success System.

I don't know how anybody could be a legal nurse consultant without taking the CLNC® Certification Program. Without it I would not have known what to do or where to begin.

Vickie taught us. Even when they gave me the job over the phone I still went in, introduced myself and made face-to-face contact. I've met all the attorneys I've worked with and know their assistants by name. When I offered to send my CV to the attorney on my latest case, he said, "That's okay. If you're good enough for Mary Sue, that's all I need." But I'll still go by and introduce myself so he'll know who he's working with.

Consistent marketing means better visibility. Because I market myself consistently, I know exactly what's in the presentation packet I send to each attorney. Even when I talk to an attorney on the phone, I can visualize what's in front of him and I can discuss my CLNC® services effectively.

I also stay visible by following up after I start my review. I call to let the attorney know what I've accomplished. That way, if there's some time between contacts, she knows I'm still out there working on the case.

The CLNC® Certification Program taught me that staying visible often presents unexpected marketing opportunities. So, as Vickie teaches us, I took some time out of my schedule to go to the courthouse to watch a malpractice case one of my defense attorney-clients was trying. During the lunch break the plaintiff attorney approached me and asked why I was there. I explained what I did, and he said, "I could have used your services on this case," which he eventually lost. I gave him my card and offered to help on his next case. Every situation is an opportunity to market and courthouses are where the attorneys are.

As a CLNC® Consultant I Set My Own Hours and Work at My Own Pace

My favorite part of being a Certified Legal Nurse Consultant℠ is reviewing the chart and determining if the standards of care have been adhered to. The Institute's training and my years of experience as a nurse give me the confidence to know I'm doing the job right. Working as a Certified Legal Nurse Consultant℠ is fascinating and exciting. I also feel like I'm making a difference by determining whether the case has merit and by educating the attorney about the medical issues of the case so he can present it to the jury in a way they can understand.

I like the independence of setting my own hours and working at my own pace. Often I'm working after my children go to sleep at night and after I take them to school during the day. This flexibility allows me to accomplish everything I need to do.

Vickie's teaching style is very entertaining and motivating, yet easy to understand. Vickie presents the CLNC® 6-Day Certification Seminar in a way that you never lose interest. When you have completed the program, you're ready to get started. She makes you believe you can do it because you're a nurse. And she's right when she says, "We are nurses and we can do anything!®"

The Institute's training and my years of experience as a nurse give me the confidence to know I'm doing the job right. Working as a Certified Legal Nurse Consultant℠ is fascinating and exciting. I also feel like I'm making a difference.

Following My Divorce I Started a New Chapter in My Life, a Chapter for *Me*

by Jeanne Enderle, APRN, FNP-BC, CLNC, Connecticut

When my marriage of 27 years ended, I had four teenagers to raise on a nurse's salary. I saw Vickie's ad and visited the LegalNurse.com website. The more I read, the more exciting legal nurse consulting sounded.

I have a clinical practice in pediatrics. I love nursing and caring for people, and I don't feel burned out with nursing. But I decided this could be a new chapter in my life, something I wanted to do for *me* personally.

I've always been a good detective. I like digging into the chart for every detail so I can understand what happened, how it happened and why it happened. And I've always been fascinated with the law and healthcare. I considered attending law school at one point. After taking Vickie Milazzo Institute's CLNC® Certification Program and seeing all the shapes justice can take, I realized that healing is a very important part of justice.

I do a lot of advocacy and volunteer work with survivors of clergy sexual abuse. Having heard hundreds of survivor stories and seeing how justice and healing fit together, I saw a role I could play as a legal nurse consultant in preparing those individuals for deposition and trial by helping them find the words to describe their experience accurately. The words can only come from them, but as a nurse, I could pick up on subtle signs and know the questions to ask. In turn, I could translate the person's answers into specific damages for the attorney. Knowing I could use my CLNC® training to delve into this area of interest played a huge part in my decision to become a Certified Legal Nurse Consultant℠.

On My First Legal Nurse Consulting Case I Kept Hearing Vickie's Voice

My first case came in the form of a call from an attorney's office looking for a nurse to testify in a case about side rails. I hadn't worked in a hospital in over 20 years. I've been a nurse practitioner for 25 of my 30 years in nursing, and while I was sure I had information the attorney needed, I wouldn't be the right person to serve as a testifying expert about side rails.

Nevertheless, I called and said, "Send me the case. I need to review it." I communicated my fee and retainer policy to the paralegal, and said I would send a letter agreement. "Ordinarily," I said, "I would speak to the attorney about this." Ordinarily? I had never done this before.

As I reviewed the records, I kept hearing Vickie say, "Make sure you address what the attorney really wants." What I wanted to talk about had nothing to do with side rails. Nevertheless, I told him, "I'll address the side rail issue, but that's the least of your worries."

The attorney told me, 'I learned more from you in 90 minutes than I learned from the neurologist who's our testifying expert from Yale.'... Being validated in this way is wonderful.

The case involved a young woman who had finished chemotherapy and was in the hospital for a blood transfusion. She had very low hemoglobin and almost zero white count. She was on anticoagulants. I noticed she was admitted on Friday afternoon. They transfused her during the night, and early the next morning they found her on the floor, fully conscious, and they were mad that she had fallen.

The nurse noted, "The patient realizes she made a mistake in getting out of bed by herself." What a self-serving note. The nurse had little to say about the injuries, claiming the patient just had a bump on the head. I was sure the woman must have had significant bruising and other injuries.

The woman vomited, lost consciousness and died of an intracerebral hemorrhage severe enough to herniate the brain. Horrified, I looked at her medications. They had continued to give her narcotic pain medication all day, even after she hit her head. She was nauseated, so they gave her Compazine. Basically, they masked every sign of increased intracranial pressure, except pupil dilation, which they only checked a couple of times.

90 Minutes Proved a CLNC® Consultant Is More Important Than an MD

When I walked the attorney through the case, he started mumbling under his breath. He clearly had no idea of the case's enormity. He later told me, "I learned more from you in 90 minutes than

I learned from the neurologist who's our testifying expert from Yale."

Before we finished talking, he asked if I knew anything about nonstress tests. I said, "Yes, I do." Then he asked if I could find an OB expert. I could hear Vickie saying, *Yes!* "Yes, I can," I said. That was my second case.

I'm in Exactly the Right Place and That's Success

Being validated in this way is wonderful. My selling point to attorneys is that I can review a case far more economically than a physician can and that my review will be broad based and in greater depth because of my nursing perspective. In addition, I will streamline the case for the medical testifying expert.

At this year's *NACLNC®* Conference, I was in the room ten minutes and I knew I was in exactly the right place. The conference is inspirational, like going to see old friends. My business is percolating because of the Certified Legal Nurse Consultant^CM training I received.

I follow cases in the newspaper, and when I know I have something to contribute, I call the attorneys involved. The first time I had sweaty hands, but I phoned the Institute and a CLNC® Mentor helped me prepare for the call. The case intrigued me. A woman had gone to an orthopedist for surgery, and he sexually assaulted her in the office. He also gave her antianxiety drugs, to which

My business is percolating because of the Certified Legal Nurse Consultant^CM training I received.

she became addicted. When I called the attorney, he said he had a doctor and nurses on staff. I told him what I had to offer was different. He listened and told me to send him my information. As the CLNC® Mentor said, "That's success."

I Have Flexible Hours, I'm Valued, I'm Validated and I Love It

When I went to the Trial Lawyers Association Conference, I made a point of walking up to a senior partner in a high-profile law firm. I was trembling, but I shook his hand and said, "I want to thank you for all you've done on behalf of survivors of clergy abuse who have the courage to take their cases forward." He looked at my name tag, and we started talking. Minutes later, his buddies were ready to go out for dinner and drinks, but we were still talking. Finally, he said, "Give me your business card. I'll call you." Without the marketing advice from Vickie's CLNC® Certification Program, I never could have done that.

I can't say enough good things about being a Certified Legal Nurse Consultant℠. My life has changed. I'm bringing my professional expertise into an arena of healing that takes great courage—clerical sexual abuse. I don't anticipate this being my specialty exclusively, but I speak and publish on the issue. I have flexible hours. I'm valued. I'm validated. And I love it.

I Turned a Humdrum Nursing Job into an Exciting New Career

by Pam Long, RN, LLC, CLNC, Utah

About a year ago I complained to my neighbor, a successful trial attorney, about my humdrum nursing job and mediocre pay. He said, "You should go into legal nurse consulting. I think you'd enjoy that." I had no idea nurses consulted with attorneys, but it made good sense. He explained how his firm worked with an independent nurse consultant and gave me her name.

The next day I called this nurse, and we talked for an hour about legal nurse consulting. She had studied Vickie Milazzo Institute's CLNC® Certification Program and she encouraged me to check out the Institute's website.

I was soon registered for the CLNC® 6-Day Certification Seminar. The program was great, and nursing once again became an exciting and challenging career for me.

I came home after the seminar and began preparing for my CLNC® business. Animated by Vickie's marketing ideas, I was determined to be successful so I worked at my business plan consistently. Before long I was networking with my attorney neighbor and I told him how Vickie's program had prepared me to meet attorneys' needs.

He was impressed that I had taken the CLNC® Certification Program and gave me a case. When I turned in my report, he was extremely pleased and

I was networking with my attorney neighbor... He was impressed that I had taken the CLNC® Certification Program and gave me a case.

I just turned in my report. If my attorney-client wins the case, he could save the corporation $10,000,000. It's obvious he's getting more than his money's worth tapping into my skills as a successful CLNC® consultant.

gave me a much more important case, the defense of a negligence suit against a huge public utilities corporation. I just turned in my 40-page comprehensive report. If my attorney-client wins the case, he could save the corporation $10,000,000. It's obvious he's getting more than his money's worth tapping into my skills as a successful CLNC® consultant.

Thanks, Vickie, for giving me the keys to success. I'm so excited about my new career path. I even convinced one of my nurse friends to become a Certified Legal Nurse Consultant[CM].

My Daughter's Case Was My First CLNC® Assignment

by Donna Berning, RN, CLNC, Oregon

O n July 31, 1991, my daughter was born with meconium aspiration that eventually caused hypoxia, leaving her with cerebral palsy. When she was seven weeks old, I started my nursing clinicals. During these rotations I learned that several key things about my daughter's care and follow-up had not been right. I hired an attorney, and the day after I graduated from nursing school, I filed suit against the doctor and the hospital.

My attorney's best friend was a nurse who worked on my daughter's case for 2½ years. Because of my stake in the outcome, I worked closely with him and found the work very interesting. Unfortunately, this nurse died of a massive MI before my case was complete.

By this time I was very discouraged about the medical field. My attorney told me about Vickie Milazzo Institute. He said that with a few years of nursing experience behind me and the knowledge I was accumulating on my own case, I could pursue both avenues.

With his advice, I ordered the CLNC® Home-Study Certification Program. I finished the course and passed the CLNC® Certification Examination.

It was my own attorney who handed me my first CLNC® assignment—my daughter's case. He said it would be hard to bring another medical person up

> *My attorney told me about Vicke Milazzo Institute.... With his advice, I ordered the CLNC® Certification Program.*

> *It was my own attorney who handed me my first CLNC® assignment.*

My business continues to grow every day. Becoming a Certified Legal Nurse Consultant[CM] *has allowed me to grow both personally and professionally, and has made me a better nurse.*

to speed on it when I knew it like the back of my hand. The medical analysis was already written, so all I had to do was attend the depositions, help answer medical-related questions, point out areas of concern, and explain lab values and reports. In January 1998, my daughter's case settled out of court.

Because I needed a steady income to care for my daughter, I kept my nursing position in the recovery room at an ambulatory center. However, I cut down to three days a week and opened my own CLNC® business working two days a week, nights and weekends.

My business continues to grow every day. Becoming a Certified Legal Nurse Consultant[CM] has allowed me to grow both personally and professionally, and has made me a better nurse. I am also in a position to help other families who are in the same situation my family is in due to the negligence of healthcare providers.

Take 5 Simple Steps to Launch Your CLNC® *Career*

by Vickie L. Milazzo, RN, MSN, JD

These nurses have shared their success stories with you for a reason. They are living a life they never could have imagined until they became Certified Legal Nurse Consultants[CM], and they want other smart, hardworking RNs like you to achieve the same success they enjoy.

If you're at a stage in your nursing career where you're ready for something different, new and exciting, I invite you to take your first easy step, today. Legal nurse consulting can be the satisfying, prosperous career you've been looking for. You are on the brink of that discovery, that success, and I share your excitement.

Certified Legal Nurse Consultants[CM] want other smart, hardworking RNs like you to achieve the same success they enjoy.

Your secret to success can be as simple as making and keeping my 5 Promises.

There has never been a better time to become a Certified Legal Nurse Consultant[CM]. Of the 1,203,097* attorneys in practice today, 25% deal with medical malpractice and personal injury cases—that's more than 225,000 possible clients for you. Not to mention tens of thousands of insurance companies and HMOs that need your CLNC® services. The potential for CLNC® consultants is unlimited. Career Builder has named legal nurse consulting as one of the Top 10 Hottest Jobs. I have never seen a more exciting, more vibrant, more fun time to start your legal nurse consulting practice than today.

One step at a time, you can make this happen for yourself. You can build a CLNC® practice that matters, that works for you and that brings you the financial rewards you deserve.

What would your life look like if every moment of it was absolutely enriched, fulfilled and swelling with joy? Think about it—your health, relationships, career, spirituality and finances are the best they can be and you greet each day with energy and enthusiasm for whatever comes your way. What would accomplish that?

My 5 Promises Can Be the Secret to Your Success

Your secret to success can be as simple as making and keeping my 5 Promises. After all, the most important promises are the ones we make to ourselves.

---

*According to the American Bar Association Market Research Department, in 2010 there were 1,203,097 attorneys in the U.S.

When I pioneered legal nurse consulting in 1982, I made 5 Promises that I've continued to make daily for more than two decades. These are not the only secrets to my success, but I know my business would not be where it is today if I hadn't kept these essential success promises. Make these promises today, and they will guide you in starting your new career as a successful Certified Legal Nurse Consultant^{CM}.

Promise 1
I will only work my passion.

We all know when we discover something we feel passionate about. We feel amazingly energetic. Desire is energy. Have you ever experienced a time when desire overcame all physical, emotional and intellectual barriers? Like a child waking up on Christmas morning, you spring alert full speed ahead. Why can't we experience that passion—that vitality and energy—not only on Christmas but every day? Believe me, you can.

When you wake up every day to a life and career you're passionate about, you experience maximum joy. Now is the time to turn on your passion for legal nurse consulting. Don't wait another day.

Promise 2
I will go for it or reject it outright.

If you want something better for your life and career, you owe it to yourself to go for it or reject it outright. Don't leave the dream dangling as a reminder of what you don't have the time, courage or enthusiasm to grab. Do it or forget it. If you want to become

> *When you wake up every day to a life and career you're passionate about, you experience maximum joy.*

> *If you want something better for your life and career, you owe it to yourself to go for it or reject it outright.*

a CLNC® consultant, don't wait for the conditions in your life to be perfect. That will never happen.

One thing that helps me overcome my career fears is perspective. Think about the worst thing that could happen if you go for it. Unless it's worse than cancer, I say, "What have I got to lose?"

It's perfectly okay to admit that a commitment is not right for you and to reject it outright. After all, this is your life, your passionate future. What's not okay is to hold back and put less than everything into a commitment that is your passion.

I have a fear of cliff-hanging heights. Despite that fear, I stepped out of an airplane at 14,000 feet to skydive. Once out of the plane, I couldn't step back in. I was truly committed. Make that kind of all-or-nothing commitment to your own career choice and you'll wake up each day to a career you love.

Promise 3
I will take one action step a day toward my career goals.

Dreams and visions are great, but without action they are nothing more than hallucinations. Without action your visions scud away and dissolve like clouds. I've met many people much smarter than I am who had dreams and ideas but didn't do anything with them. They didn't take action.

I created a new profession and led thousands of nurses to success. I accomplished that goal with *one action step at a time.* I had to take action every day to build the momentum necessary to live my career dreams. By taking action every day you develop the habit and discipline to make your vision a reality.

Where you focus is where you will yield results. When you focus not just on the idea but on making it happen, you stay in motion, not just dreaming your passions but living them.

If you want big results, you must guard your time carefully and focus on Big Things. Every day, take at least one action step on the Big Thing that brings you closer to CLNC® success.

Promise 4
I commit to being a success student for life.

Success breeds success. Becoming a success student for life is about practicing being successful. What's hard today is easy tomorrow—with practice. I've been in business for over two decades, and I still learn every day—from my students, staff members, favorite writers, speakers and successful CEOs. There are two ways to learn:

- ▶ The hard way—through trial and error, making lots of mistakes.
- ▶ The easy way—through the right mentor who has already achieved success. No matter what problem you encounter, the CLNC® Mentors and I have already successfully managed a challenge just like it.

No matter what the subject, there's always more to learn. Commit now to being a lifetime student and to learning not only from your own mistakes and accomplishments but also from successful CLNC® Mentors.

Where you focus is where you will yield results.... If you want big results, you must guard your time carefully and focus on Big Things.

Promise 5
I believe as a nurse I really can do anything.

Any time I have hesitated to take action toward living my dream, it was because I had stopped believing in myself. Today, when an opportunity arises and I find myself hesitating, I remember, "I am a nurse and nurses can do anything!"

Think about your ability to make split-second decisions that are the difference between life and death for your patients. Remind yourself: "If I can save lives in the middle of the night while the rest of the world is sleeping and an MD is nowhere in sight, surely I can succeed as a CLNC® consultant."

Honor yourself daily with this fact: "I am a nurse and I can do anything!"

This proven life plan works. And it's easy. Apply these 5 success promises today. I guarantee your life will become an adventure more powerful, satisfying and fun than you can imagine.

Embrace your amazing new career without limits today.

Promise BIG and promise NOW!

Vickie L. Milazzo, RN, MSN, JD
The Pioneer of Legal Nurse Consulting

Adapted from Wicked Success Is Inside Every Woman *(published by John Wiley & Sons, Inc.), available wherever books are sold.*

> *Remind yourself: 'If I can save lives in the middle of the night while the rest of the world is sleeping and an MD is nowhere in sight, surely I can succeed as a CLNC® consultant.'*

About the ℰditor

Vickie L. Milazzo, RN, MSN, JD

Inc. Top 10 Entrepreneur and *New York Times* bestselling author Vickie L. Milazzo, RN, MSN, JD is founder and president of Vickie Milazzo Institute. Vickie single-handedly pioneered the field of legal nurse consulting in 1982. According to *The New York Times*, she "crossed nursing with the law and created a new profession." Her master's degree in nursing, with a concentration in education, and her law degree uniquely qualified Vickie to invent this profitable career opportunity for registered nurses.

Vickie Changed the Face of Nursing

Named by *Inc.* magazine as one of the Top 5000 Fastest-Growing Private Companies in America, the Institute is the oldest and largest legal nurse consulting training institute and the only publishing company exclusively devoted to this field. Vickie created the trademark CLNC® Certification

Program, the first national legal nurse consulting certification. She then built the *National Alliance of Certified Legal Nurse Consultants* (*NACLNC*®), a professional association of 5,000 members. Nationally recognized by attorneys, the CLNC® Certification is the official certification of the *NACLNC*® Association.

Vickie has trained, coached and mentored more than 22,000 RNs as Certified Legal Nurse Consultants[CM], empowering them to take control of their lives, create exciting nursing careers and achieve financial freedom. She is recognized as the nation's expert on legal nurse consulting and as a dynamic role model by tens of thousands of nurses. Her company was named by *Inc.* magazine as one of the Top 50 Education Companies in America. Vickie teaches the innovative business strategies that changed the face of nursing and earned her a place on the national list of *Inc.* Top 10 Entrepreneurs.

New York Times Bestselling Author Defines the Standards for Legal Nurse Consulting

Vickie is the author of the national bestsellers *Core Curriculum for Legal Nurse Consulting*® textbook, the CLNC® Certification Program; the Private and *NACLNC*® Apprenticeships; *I Am a Successful CLNC*® *Success Journal*; *Create Your Own Magic for CLNC*® *Success, Second Edition*; and *Flash 55 Promotions: 55 FREE Ways to Promote Your CLNC*® *Business, Second Edition*. She is a contributor to the *Nursing Leadership Encyclopedia* and is coauthor of several books: *101 Great Ways to*

Improve Your Life; *Rising to the Top* coauthored with Jim Rohn and Jack Canfield; and *Roadmap to Success* coauthored with Ken Blanchard and Stephen Covey. Vickie is the author of *Vickie's Legal Nurse Consulting Blog* at LegalNurse.com/VickiesBlog. She successfully engages her legal nurse consulting audience, students and Certified Legal Nurse Consultants^{CM} with up-to-the-minute news and information on her more than 300-page LegalNurse.com website and through Facebook, LinkedIn and Twitter.

She is the author of *The New York Times* bestseller *Wicked Success Is Inside Every Woman*, published by John Wiley & Sons, Inc. Vickie's *Inside Every Woman* seminars, delivered across the country, are available on DVDs and CDs.

As the authoritative educator in her field, Vickie has been featured or profiled in numerous publications, including *The New York Times*, *Women's Health*, *St. Louis Post-Dispatch*, *Success*, *Houston Woman Magazine*, *NurseWeek*, *Entrepreneur*, *Small Business Success*, *Cincinnati Enquirer*, *Houston Chronicle*, *Investor's Business Daily*, *Pittsburgh Business Times*, *Ladies Home Journal*™, *Texas Bar Journal*, Knight Ridder Media Services, *Los Angeles Times*, *Philadelphia Inquirer*, *Working Nurse*, *Baltimore Sun*, *Fort Worth Star-Telegram*, various Gannett publications and in more than 220 newspapers reaching 16.6 million readers.

Her work has been published everywhere from *USA Today* and *Seventeen* to *PINK* magazine and in many nursing, legal and business media, such as

MSNBC.com, StartupNation.com, *Lawyers USA*, *Nursing Spectrum*, *Forensic Nurse*, *American Journal of Nursing*, *National Medical-Legal Reporter*, *Association of Trial Lawyers of America Newsletter* and *Entrepreneur's StartUps*.

A nationally acclaimed keynote speaker and member of the National Speakers Association, Vickie has spoken for groups such as the American Association for Justice, The Oprah Winfrey Boys & Girls Club, Texas Trial Lawyers Association, Farmers Insurance, Oncology Nursing Society, eWomen Network, the Kripalu Center for Yoga and Health and other business and professional organizations. Vickie has presented a national conference on leadership strategies for women with CEO and *New York Times* bestselling author Stedman Graham. She has also educated thousands of nurses as an Internet chat host.

Vickie's Nationwide Media Attention Spotlights the CLNC® Profession

Vickie has appeared on national radio and TV as an expert on legal nurse consulting, entrepreneurship and career advancement. As a contributor to the National Public Radio program, *This I Believe®*, she shared her success strategies with NPR listeners. NPR has an audience of more than 26 million listeners. She has also been featured on over 200 other national and local radio stations, reaching more than 20 million listeners, including XM Satellite Radio, Sirius Satellite Radio, KMAZ (Los Angeles), WONX (Chicago), WWAM (Philadelphia), WKNH (Boston) and WFNY (NYC). Vickie's television appearances include ABC, CBS, FOX, NBC, Bloomberg TV, At Home Live, Better TV (New York), Great Day Houston, The CEO Show and dozens more.

Awards and Recognition

Vickie's many honors include:

- *New York Times* Bestselling Author
- *Inc.* Top 10 Entrepreneur–one of the top 10 entrepreneurs in the U.S.
- *Inc.* Top 5000 Fastest-Growing Private Company in America
- *Inc.* Top 50 Fastest-Growing Education Company in America
- Stevie® Award (Business's Oscar®)–Mentor of the Year
- *Wall Street Journal* Bestselling Author
- *Inc.* Bestselling Business Author
- Most Innovative Small Business by Pitney Bowes®
- Top 100 Small Business in Houston
- Top 25 Woman-Owned Business in Houston
- Top 50 Fastest-Growing Woman-Owned Business in Houston
- Telly Award for DVD Presentation Production
- Top 50 Most Influential Woman in Houston
- *NurseWeek* Nursing Excellence Award for Advancing the Profession

▸ Susan G. Komen's Hope Award for Ambassadorship

Vickie earned her bachelor of science in nursing at the University of St. Thomas and her master of science in nursing at Texas Woman's University, both in Houston. She earned her juris doctor at South Texas College of Law.

Mentor of the Year Transforms Careers

In all her work Vickie openly shares her practical and proven strategies as she coaches and mentors nurses to take charge of their professional destiny. Her audiences are transformed and inspired to action by her extensive business expertise, irresistible drive and vibrant energy. Vickie is a powerful advocate for women in business and for nurses.

Vickie's vision is to revolutionize nursing careers one RN at a time. The most common refrain from nurses attending her seminars and conferences is, *"She changed my life!"*

You Can Add Your Own CLNC® Success Story to Our
Collection of Thousands

"My CLNC® Success Story"

_____
_____
_____
_____
_____
_____
_____
_____
_____
_____
_____
_____
_____
_____
_____
_____
_____
_____
_____
_____
_____
_____
_____
_____

Send your CLNC® Success Story to: Vickie Milazzo Institute, 5615 Kirby Drive, Suite 425, Houston, TX 77005 or email to mail@LegalNurse.com. Your CLNC® Success Story may be considered for a future edition of this book.